UNDERSTANDING
JAMES DICKEY

Understanding Contemporary
American Literature

Matthew J. Bruccoli, *Editor*

Understanding Bernard Malamud by Jeffrey Helterman
Understanding James Dickey by Ronald Baughman
Understanding John Hawkes by Donald J. Greiner

UNDERSTANDING
James
DICKEY

BY RONALD BAUGHMAN

UNIVERSITY OF SOUTH CAROLINA PRESS

Cover Photograph of James Dickey
by Terry Parke

Copyright © University of South Carolina 1985

First Edition

Published in Columbia, South Carolina, by the University of South Carolina Press

Manufactured in the United States of America

Library of Congress Cataloging-in-Publication Data

Baughman, Ronald, 1940–
  Understanding James Dickey.

  (Understanding contemporary American literature)
  Bibliography: p.
  Includes index.
  1. Dickey, James—Criticism and interpretation.
I. Title. II. Series.
PS3554.I32Z56 1985   811'.54   85–16532
ISBN 0–87249–472–1 (pbk.)
ISBN 0–87249–471–3

For
Velma A. Baughman
and
Judith S. Baughman
and
Elizabeth Smith Baughman

CONTENTS

EDITOR'S PREFACE

Understanding Contemporary American Literature has been planned as a series of guides or companions for students as well as good nonacademic readers. The editor and publisher perceive a need for these volumes because much of the influential contemporary literature makes special demands. Uninitiated readers encounter difficulty in approaching works that depart from the traditional forms and techniques of prose and poetry. Literature relies on conventions, but the conventions keep evolving; new writers form their own conventions—which in time may become familiar. Put simply, *UCAL* provides instruction in how to read certain contemporary writers—identifying and explicating their material, themes, use of language, point of view, structures, symbolism, and responses to experience.

The word *understanding* in the series title was deliberately chosen. Many willing readers lack an adequate understanding of how contemporary literature works; that is, what the author is attempting to express and the means by which it is conveyed. Although the criticism and analysis in the series have

EDITOR'S PREFACE

been aimed at a level of general accessibility, these introductory volumes are meant to be applied in conjunction with the works they cover. Thus they do not provide a substitute for the works and authors they introduce, but rather prepare the reader for more profitable literary experiences.

M. J. B.

ACKNOWLEDGMENTS

I gratefully thank the University of South Carolina's Research and Productive Scholarship Committee for a grant that allowed me access to certain research material.

ACKNOWLEDGMENTS

University Press. This poem first appeared in *The New Yorker.*

"The Owl King." Copyright © 1962 by James Dickey. Reprinted from *Poems 1957–1967* by permission of Wesleyan University Press.

"In the Mountain Tent." Copyright © 1961 by James Dickey. Reprinted from *Poems 1957–1967* by permission of Wesleyan University Press. This poem first appeared in *The New Yorker.*

"Horses and Prisoners." Copyright © 1963 by James Dickey. Reprinted from *Poems 1957–1967* by permission of Wesleyan University Press.

"The Driver." Copyright © 1963 by James Dickey. Reprinted from *Poems 1957–1967* by permission of Wesleyan University Press. This poem first appeared in *The New Yorker.*

"Drinking from a Helmet." Copyright © 1963 by James Dickey. Reprinted from *Poems 1957–1967* by permission of Wesleyan University Press.

"Approaching Prayer." Copyright © 1964 by James Dickey. Reprinted from *Poems 1957–1967* by permission of Wesleyan University Press.

"Cherrylog Road." Copyright © 1963 by James Dickey. Reprinted from *Poems 1957–1967* by permission of Wesleyan University Press. This poem first appeared in *The New Yorker.*

"Chenille." Copyright © 1964 by James Dickey. Reprinted from *Poems 1957–1967* by permission of Wesleyan University Press.

"Springer Mountain." Copyright © 1962 by James Dickey. Reprinted from *Poems 1957–1967* by permission of Wesleyan University Press.

"Kudzu." Copyright © 1963 by James Dickey. Reprinted from *Poems 1957–1967* by permission of Wesleyan University Press. This poem first appeared in *The New Yorker.*

"The Ice Skin." Copyright © 1963 by James Dickey. Reprinted from *Poems 1957–1967* by permission of Wesleyan University Press. This poem first appeared in *The New Yorker.*

"The Firebombing." Copyright © 1964 by James Dickey. Reprinted from *Poems 1957–1967* by permission of Wesleyan University Press. This poem first appeared in *Poetry.*

"Buckdancer's Choice." Copyright © 1965 by James Dickey. Reprinted from *Poems 1957–1967* by permission of Wesleyan University Press. This poem first appeared in *The New Yorker.*

"Angina." Copyright © 1964 by James Dickey. Reprinted from *Poems 1957–1967* by permission of Wesleyan University Press. This poem first appeared in *The New Yorker.*

"Slave Quarters." Copyright © 1965 by James Dickey. Reprinted from *Poems 1957–1967* by permission of Wesleyan University Press. This poem first appeared in *The New Yorker.*

"Them, Crying." Copyright © 1964 by James Dickey. Reprinted from *Poems 1957–1967* by permission of Wesleyan

ACKNOWLEDGMENTS

University Press. This poem first appeared in *The New Yorker.*

"The Fiend." Copyright © 1965 by James Dickey. Reprinted from *Poems 1957–1967* by permission of Wesleyan University Press.

"The Shark's Parlor." Copyright © 1965 by James Dickey. Reprinted from *Poems 1957–1967* by permission of Wesleyan University Press. This poem first appeared in *The New Yorker.*

"Reincarnation (II)." Copyright © 1964 by James Dickey. Reprinted from *Poems 1957–1967* by permission of Wesleyan University Press.

"The Bee." Copyright © 1966 by James Dickey. Reprinted from *Poems 1957–1967* by permission of Wesleyan University Press.

"Bread." Copyright © 1967 by James Dickey. Reprinted from *Poems 1957–1967* by permission of Wesleyan University Press.

"Adultery." Copyright © 1966 by James Dickey. Reprinted from *Poems 1957–*

1967 by permission of Wesleyan University Press.

"The Sheep Child." Copyright © 1966 by James Dickey. Reprinted from *Poems 1957–1967* by permission of Wesleyan University Press.

"Power and Light." Copyright © 1967 by James Dickey. Reprinted from *Poems 1957–1967* by permission of Wesleyan University Press. This poem first appeared in *The New Yorker.*

"For the Last Wolverine." Copyright © 1966 by James Dickey. Reprinted from *Poems 1957–1967* by permission of Wesleyan University Press.

"May Day Sermon to the Women of Gilmer County, Georgia, by a Woman Preacher Leaving the Baptist Church." Copyright © 1967 by James Dickey. Reprinted from *Poems 1957–1967* by permission of Wesleyan University Press.

"Falling." Copyright © 1967 by James Dickey. Reprinted from *Poems 1957–1967* by permission of Wesleyan University Press. This poem first appeared in *The New Yorker.*

Excerpts from "Victory" copyright © 1968 by *The Atlantic*; from "Sugar," "The Cancer Match," and "Pine" copyright © 1969 by Modern Poetry Association; from "For the First Manned Moon Orbit" and "The Moon Ground" copyright © 1969 by Time, Inc.; from "Looking for the Buckhead Boys" copyright © 1969 by The Atlantic Monthly Company; from "Pine,"* "Turning Away," "Knock,"* "Butterflies,"* "Giving a Son to the Sea,"* "Living There," "Mercy," and "The Eye-Beaters" copyright © 1966, 1968, 1969, 1970 by James Dickey. Reprinted from *The Eye-Beaters, Blood, Victory, Madness, Buckhead and Mercy* by James Dickey.

Excerpts from "Strength of Fields," "Voyage of the Needle," "Haunting the Maneuvers," "Drums Where I Live,"* "Reunioning Dialogue," "The Rain Guitar,"* and "Remnant Water"* copyright © 1969, 1972, 1973, 1977, 1978, 1979 by James Dickey. Reprinted from *The Strength of Fields* by James Dickey.

ACKNOWLEDGMENTS

Excerpts from "The Surround" copyright © 1980 by The Atlantic Monthly Company; from "Deborah as Scion" and "From Time" copyright © 1981 by *MSS Magazine*; from "Deborah Burning a Doll" copyright © 1981 by Modern Poetry Association; from "Door Step," "Ray Flowers II," "The Lode," and "Deborah in Mountain Sound" copyright © 1982 by *The Kenyon Review*; from "Summons" copyright © 1982 by *Graham House Review*. Reprinted from *Puella* by James Dickey.

Poems marked with asterisks first appeared in *The New Yorker.*

All excerpts from poems from *The Eye-Beaters, Blood, Victory, Madness, Buckhead and Mercy, The Strength of Fields,* and *Puella* are reprinted by permission of Doubleday & Company, Inc.

UNDERSTANDING
JAMES DICKEY

CHAPTER ONE

Understanding
James Dickey

Career

J ames Dickey launched his career as a poet surprisingly late in life. His first collection, *Into the Stone and Other Poems*, was published when he was thirty-seven years old. Dickey's experience in the military, academic, and advertising worlds before his emergence as a writer provided subjects and training for his art.

Born on 2 February 1923 in Buckhead, Georgia, an Atlanta suburb, to lawyer Eugene Dickey and his wife, Maibelle Swift Dickey, James Dickey graduated from North Fulton High School (recalled with Buckhead itself in "Looking for the Buckhead Boys"). In 1941 he entered Clemson A & M College, where he played wingback on the football team. The following year he joined the Army Air Corps and as a member of the 418th Night Fighter Squadron was involved in more than one hundred bombing missions in the South Pacific.

After World War II, Dickey attended Vanderbilt University, from which he received a B.A. in English magna cum laude in 1949 and an M.A. in English in 1950. While at Vanderbilt he published four poems in the campus literary magazine, *The Gadfly*, and one—"The Shark at the Window"—in the *Sewanee Review*. During his undergraduate years he married Maxine Syerson, with whom he had two sons—Christopher, born in 1951, and Kevin, born in 1958.

Dickey's first teaching position, at Rice Institute in Houston, was interrupted when he was recalled by the Air Force for service in Korea. Following his discharge he returned to Rice but left there in 1954 to travel and write in Europe on a *Sewanee Review* fellowship. A 1956 teaching appointment in the University of Florida English department was cut short when Dickey resigned because of a dispute over his reading of his poem "The Father's Body." In April 1956 he began a successful career as copywriter and executive for advertising agencies in New York and Atlanta. During his years as an ad man Dickey continued writing poetry, for which he received several awards, including *Poetry's* Union League Civic and Arts Foundation Prize in 1958 and both the Longview Foundation Award and the Vachel Lindsay Prize in 1959.

During the 1960s Dickey began to flourish as a poet-teacher. Following the publication of *Into the Stone* in 1960 he won a Guggenheim Fellowship, which allowed him to spend 1961–62 writing in Italy. *Drowning with Others* appeared in 1962; *Helmets* and a collection of reviews and essays, *The Suspect in Poetry*, in 1964; and *Buckdancer's Choice* in 1965. For *Buckdancer's Choice* he received the 1966 National Book Award for poetry. During this period Dickey also served as poet-in-residence at several colleges and universities: Reed College (1963–64), San Fernando Valley State College

UNDERSTANDING JAMES DICKEY

(1964–65), and the University of Wisconsin at Madison (1966–67). From 1966 to 1968 he was Consultant in Poetry for the Library of Congress. *Poems 1957–1967* was published in 1967 and *Babel to Byzantium: Poets and Poetry Now* in 1968. In 1969 Dickey became professor of English and writer-in-residence at the University of South Carolina, a position he still holds.

The 1970s saw Dickey experimenting with a wide range of genres. In 1970 his novel, *Deliverance*, the collection *The Eye-Beaters, Blood, Victory, Madness, Buckhead and Mercy*, and a volume of essays, *Self-Interviews*, were published, followed the next year by *Sorties*, a journal and new essays. In 1972 he acted as script writer and consultant for the movie version of *Deliverance*, which won several Academy Award nominations and in which he played the role of Sheriff Bullard. *Jericho: The South Beheld*, with text by Dickey and paintings by Hubert Shuptrine, appeared in 1974. Dickey wrote the script for the television production of Jack London's *The Call of the Wild* in 1975, and in 1976 he published the long poem *The Zodiac*. That same year Maxine Dickey died, and Dickey married Deborah Dodson, with whom he had a daughter, Bronwen, in 1981.

During 1977 he read "The Strength of Fields," a poem commissioned for the ceremonies, at President Jimmy Carter's inauguration. That year he also published *God's Images*, which included his text and Marvin Hayes's engravings for Bible episodes. *Tucky the Hunter*, a children's poem, appeared in 1978, and the collection *The Strength of Fields* in 1979.

UNDERSTANDING JAMES DICKEY

Puella, five poems of which had earlier won the Levinson Prize, was published in 1982, followed by *Night Hurdling: Poems, Essays, Conversations, Commencements, and Afterwords* in 1983. Dickey is presently at work on his second novel, *Alnilam*.

Overview

James Dickey is a writer of extraordinary intelligence and power. He has experimented with a variety of forms—novel, personal essays, literary criticism, television and movie scripts, and poetry—and he has assumed a number of roles, among them soldier, athlete, archer, guitarist, teacher, and writer. Yet, as the novelist George Garrett has noted, to find where James Dickey truly lives, one should turn to his poetry.[1]

Garrett's comment is an accurate one, for Dickey believes strongly that the poet's personality and his work cannot and should not be separated. Indeed, at the center of each Dickey poem is a figure whom the writer labels the Self, the character through which he explores his world. Dickey's Self does not, like the protagonists of such other contemporary poets as John Berryman, Anne Sexton, and Robert Lowell, passively suffer—even luxuriate in—private flaws and downfalls; rather, this personality aggressively confronts forces that require his taking risks. An involved participant who certainly endures as much pain as the protagonists of other writers, Dickey's Self attempts to meet such challenges rather than simply succumbing to them.

In *Babel to Byzantium: Poets and Poetry Now* (1968), Dickey emphasizes the importance of his own experiences in defining the perspective of his literary Self:

What I have always striven for is to find some way to incarnate my best moments—those which in memory are most persistent and obsessive. I find that most of these moments have an element of danger, an element of repose, and an element of joy. I should like now to develop a writing instrument which would be capable of embodying these moments and their attendant states of mind, and I would be most pleased if readers came away from my poems not at all sure as to where the danger and the repose separate, where joy ends and longing begins. Strongly mixed emotions are what I usually have and what I usually remember from the events of my life. Strongly mixed, but giving the impression of being one emotion, impure and overwhelming—that is the condition I am seeking to impose on my readers, whoever they may be.[2]

Here Dickey clearly reveals that important events in his life—"those [moments] which in memory are most persistent and obsessive"—do influence the subject matter of his work. Significant too is his statement that his art, like the real-life experiences that inform it, should elicit a complex mixture of emotional responses. The true artist, he suggests, should strive for multiple effects rather than simple, reductive conclusions in setting forth his vision.

Certainly the most dramatic occurrence in Dickey's life was his involvement in Army Air Force bombing missions during World War II. Throughout his poetry and his nonfiction prose he treats the influence of war upon those who have directly experienced it. On the one hand, he concedes the elevating nature of combat, as his statement in *Self-Interviews* (1970) reveals: "There is a God-like feeling about fighting on our planet. It's useless to deny it. . . . You can never do anything in your life that will give you such a feeling of consequence and of performing a dangerous and essential part in a great cause as fighting in a world war."[3] On the other hand, he also suggests that to have fought and survived a war leaves an imprint of a very different sort on the veteran: "In World War II I was in some awfully harrowing action in the Pacific, and in some places I didn't think it would be possible to survive at all. The result is that now, far removed from those scenes, places, and events, I view existence pretty much from the standpoint of a survivor—sort of like a perpetual convalescent."[4]

Dickey returns to this idea in *Sorties* (1971): "More and more I see myself as the poet of *survival*."[5] These statements provide an important key—perhaps the most important key—to his work. His encounters with death through war came when he was a very young man. Upon his return to civilian life he brought the perspective of the war survivor to his relationships with family, friends, society in general, and nature.

UNDERSTANDING JAMES DICKEY

Throughout his work Dickey engages in a process of self-exploration founded upon his vision of himself as a survivor.

The process is perhaps most fully defined by Robert Jay Lifton in *Home from the War*. While his study focuses on the war survivor, Lifton correctly asserts that what is true for the specific experience of combat also holds true for any deeply felt death encounter. He observes that most combat veterans feel a "death imprint" referred to broadly as "survivor's guilt." One who survives a war may believe that his life has been saved because someone else has died in his place. Yet even as he suffers the agony of losing close friends, the war veteran experiences a grateful relief, even joy, at his own survival; such contradictory emotions produce his guilt, an enormous "turning inward of anger." This anger, Lifton determines, usually causes the survivor to feel two successive forms of guilt, the "static" and the "animating."

Static guilt is characterized by psychic numbing—a kind of emotional paralysis, a "self-laceration"—which causes the veteran to have difficulty in making emotional investments in himself or others. In order to move to animating guilt, which offers a measure of "self-knowledge" or "self-illumination," the survivor goes through three stages in a "symbolic form of death and rebirth": first, he experiences "confrontation," "a sudden or sustained questioning . . . brought about by some form of death encounter"; next, he undergoes a "reordering" of his perceptions about the dead, a "breaking down of some of the character armor, the long-standing defenses and maneuvers around numbed guilt"; and, finally, he accomplishes a "renewal," a feeling that he can now be "the author of [his] own life story."⁶

Lifton's three stages in the progression from static to animating guilt—confrontation, reordering, and renewal—help define the development of Dickey's work. The poet moves from an initial uncertainty to an eventual measure of order in understanding not only his combat involvement but also his wider range of relationships and experiences. Thus, as he treats his major subjects—war, family, love, social man, and nature—the writer is working out his constantly evolving perspective as a survivor.

In his first collection, *Into the Stone and Other Poems* (1960), Dickey suggests the nature of the death imprint left on him by his combat experiences. He notes, for example, in "The Jewel" that he is still strongly attracted to war's machinery but that he cannot now determine if he has truly survived war's destruction. He feels suspended between the world of the living and the world of the dead. Such a suspension also characterizes his relationships in this volume with his family, particularly with his dead older brother, Eugene; Dickey's efforts to connect with Eugene in "The String," "The Underground Stream," and "The Other" are thwarted. His attempt to defeat death through love achieves success in "Into the Stone"; but when he moves to nature, as in "Sleeping Out at Easter" and "The Vegetable King," he again seems uncertain about whether the forces of life or death prevail in him.

Consequently, in his second volume, *Drowning with Others* (1962), Dickey explores the condition of the dead. He tries to duplicate the experience of those who have died in "The Island," and he dramatizes the imprisonment—a psychological death—of former comrades and former enemies in "Between Two Prisoners." Examining the possibility that each person has the potential for achieving kingly, angel-like stature in "The Owl King," he suggests that the failure of that potential—shown in "The Lifeguard"—induces lacerating guilt, deathlike despair. "In the Tree House at Night" reveals the poet balanced between the worlds of the dead and the living. Since he cannot reach either location through man's environment, he again turns to nature in "The Heaven of Animals," wherein the hunter-hunted relationship perfects the cycle of killing and being killed without guilt. Yet this is a world whose values he, as a human being, is unable to adopt.

In Dickey's third volume, *Helmets* (1964), he discovers a means of providing personal protection and concealment from the forces of death and remorse. The various helmets he dons allow him such protection, yet they also function as a means of communication with the dead. By putting on a helmet, as he does in "Drinking from a Helmet," the poet gains the dead's last thoughts and feelings. Such knowledge advances his process of assuming control over his survivor's guilt, for now he experiences a reordering knowledge about the war dead. At the same time, through the use of the helmet he acquires a means of communication with others who are not war casualties: in "Approaching Prayer" he wins insight into his father's and his own lives; in "Springer Mountain" he connects with nature; in "The Scarred Girl" he discovers an affection for inner beauty; in "Cherrylog Road" he suggests some of the renewing power of love. The helmet thus aids him both in concealing himself from death and guilt and in approaching their mysteries.

After he has clarified his insights into the dead, particularly the war dead, the poet is ready in *Buckdancer's Choice* (1965), his fourth collection, to raise questions about the nature of his survivor's guilt. In "The Firebombing," for example, he asks whether he should be absolved or sentenced for his war actions, but can come to no easy conclusion. The same is true of his family poems in the volume: both "Buckdancer's Choice" and "Angina" explore his highly ambiguous relationship with his mother. Furthermore, this ambivalence carries over into his treatment of other figures from society at large: the Southern slavemaster in "Slave Quarters"; the voyeur in "The Fiend"; the teen-aged boy in "The Shark's Parlor." In each case their creator is unable—and unwilling—simply to absolve or sentence them.

The collection *Falling*, which had its first book publication in *Poems 1957–1967* (1967), marks Dickey's initial acknowledgment that guilt may, in fact, be animating, may provide an avenue toward renewal. In "Adultery" he declares, "Guilt is magical," and suggests that, put in proper perspective, it may expand rather than limit the survivor's vision of his life. Throughout *Falling*—in the title poem, in "Reincarnation (II)," in "The Bee," in "Power and Light," to cite only a few examples—there are repeated images of protagonists rising to or falling from the possibilities of renewed life. Although the risks taken do not always meet with success, the speakers' efforts suggest potential for animating guilt.

The same current exists in *The Eye-Beaters, Blood, Victory, Madness, Buckhead and Mercy* (1970), although in this volume the tone is quite different. Instead of focusing on figures who are clearly not himself, the poet turns inward, portraying a speaker who seems to have clear autobiographical elements. A middle-aged, sometimes ill, always reflective man, this figure reveals in such poems as "Diabetes" and "The Cancer Match" his awareness that man's hold on life is precarious. Furthermore, in "Messages" and "Two Poems of Going Home" he emphasizes his sense that both his family and his concept of home will slip away from him. In the war poem "Victory" and the love poem "Mercy" he suggests the fusion of death and life. Finally, in "Turning Away," the volume's concluding poem, he declares that in order to achieve his renewal, his new life, he must "change" and "form again."

This goal Dickey ultimately achieves in *Deliverance* (1970), his only novel to date. In this more expansive form the writer probes in detail the development of a central character whose experiences clearly reflect those endured in combat. Ed Gentry, who describes himself as a "get-through-the-day man," initially feels little consequence in his life. However, through a series of kill-or-be-killed death encounters in the wilderness, he is forced to act and then to weigh his actions. In so doing he is able to save himself, to attain a new life in and outside the wilderness, to become—in Lifton's word—"author" of that life.

The sense of renewal achieved in *Deliverance* clearly affects the tone, the voices, the techniques in the collections following the novel. *The Zodiac* (1976) and *Puella* (1982) point new directions for Dickey. Each work brings forth a unique speaking voice—that of Hendrik Marsman, a drunken Dutch poet observed by an omniscient "I" narrator, and that of Deborah, a young woman "male imagined"; furthermore, each volume alters the expected narrative form or abandons it altogether. But in each the central figure—Marsman or Deborah—seems to achieve affirmation. *The Strength of Fields* (1979), a collection which is closer in subject matter and technique to Dickey's earlier works, displays a Self that appears kinder and more reconciled than that in the pre-*Deliverance* works. In all three of these later volumes Dickey seems to have replaced self-lacerating guilt with self-animating guilt and thus to have won renewal.

As he moves from confrontation through reordering to renewal, Dickey constantly employs a special process—"the way of exchange of identity"—defined early in the poet's career by H. L. Weatherby.[7] As Weatherby shows, to move outside of a restrictive Self the writer exchanges his identity with that of another being or object, the Other, which provides an actual and symbolic contrast to the Self. He may adopt the character of an animal (an owl in *Deliverance*, a boar in "Approaching Prayer," a dog in "A Dog Sleeping on My Feet") or of an inanimate object (a mountain in *Deliverance*, a pine tree in "Pine"). He may gain the perspective of one of the dead (a soldier in "Drinking from a Helmet" or his dead brother in "Armor"), of a family member (a child in "To His Children in Darkness"), or of another human being (a passing stranger in "Faces Seen Once" or a voyeur in "The Fiend"). These exchanges of identity give the poet a different point of view on the world, a point of view that aids in informing and transforming the Self.

The dramatic tension between the Self and the Other also enhances the story element in the poems, and Dickey is, in most of his best work, a narrative poet. As he comments in *Sorties,*

Somebody said of my poetry that it attempts to win back for poetry some of the territory that poetry has unnecessarily relinquished to the novel. That is accurate. I like very much the emphasis on narrative that this implies, but above all the emphasis on *action* of some kind. . . . It must be a completed action, and the plunging in of the reader into this action is the most difficult and the most desirable feat that the poet can perform.[8]

The individual works are frequently circular in structure; that is, the ending of a poem brings it back to its beginning. As George Lensing points out in "The Neo-Romanticism of James Dickey," this circularity is particularly noticeable in the poet's treatment of setting: he first establishes its real-world components; he then enters and reconstructs it through his "personal egocentric vision"; he finally reestablishes the original setting at the conclusion of the poem.[9] This movement also clearly applies to—but is expanded in—the process the Self undergoes. Encountering a clear predicament, the Self exchanges identity with the Other and finally returns to its starting point. Yet, as Weatherby suggests, the Self normally undergoes a change, a transformation, because of its exchange with the Other.[10]

Dickey's treatment of the evolution of the Self has generated a set of repeated symbols, most of them associated with nature. Because the action of many of his poems occurs at night, the moon plays a special role in endowing his speakers—as in "The Owl King"—with unique visionary powers denied them during their rational, daylight hours. (Indeed, sight/blindness is a major motif throughout Dickey's work.) The urge toward celestial beings and powers also appears in the poet's use of mythological figures (the star formations in "For the Nightly Ascent of the Hunter Orion" and *The Zodiac*) and of magically endowed birds of prey (the sea bird in "Reincarnation (II)," the owls in "The Owl King" and *Deliverance*). Water, traditionally associated with rebirth, assumes additional complexity in Dickey's work. In *Deliverance*, to cite only one example, it functions as both a renewing and a destructive element; in the latter capacity it shares some of the features of the shark and the snake, the poet's persistent emblems of impersonal, unyielding malevolence.

The most complex of Dickey's symbolic creations is his underworld of the dead, to which water often leads. For him the dead have a physical reality, and they involve themselves with the living as sometimes helpful, sometimes hostile intruders; the godlike specter of Eugene in "The Other," for instance, both inspires and intimidates the speaker. In his interview with William Heyen, Dickey states, "I tried to fathom what it [death] was, what death is essentially. I finally decided that it's being in the ultimate strange place, the thing that's most completely different from what you're accustomed to."[11] In his underworld the dead reside in a Hadeslike location "Below the surface of thought / Below the ground," as he describes it in "The Signs."[12] Its similarity to the Greek underworld in its location, its humanizing of the dead souls, and its underground rivers, lakes, and streams is apparent. Because the dead embody the causes for the speaker's guilt, they serve as haunting presences impelling the poet's attempts to break away from or transform the Self.

In order to convey his vision Dickey has, of course, devised appropriate poetic techniques. The poems of his first three collections—*Into the Stone, Drowning with Others,* and *Helmets*—tend to be organized into recognizable stanzaic units. Many of these poems feature italicized refrains—lines that are repeated, or perhaps slightly altered, at the end of each stanza—to help unify the individual works. "The String," for example, employs variations on the refrain *"Dead before I was born"*[13] to suggest the extent to which the speaker's dead brother preys on his mind. When rhyme is used (it is infrequent in the early collections and virtually nonexistent in the later ones), it is generally "slant" or "off" rhyme, as in these lines from "The Underground Stream":

> I lay at the edge of a well,
> And thought how to bury my smile

> Under the thorn, where the leaf,
> At the still of oblivion safe,
> Put forth its instant green
> In a flow from underground.[14]

This passage also illustrates Dickey's favorite metrical devices in these early volumes: a three-beat line composed primarily of anapestic ($\smile\smile-$) feet with frequent iambic ($\smile-$) or trochaic ($-\smile$) substitutions.

Beginning with *Buckdancer's Choice*, Dickey increasingly experiments with a less traditional, more complex form, which he has labeled the "open" poem. Spreading out over the page to create a visual openness, this form also uses spaces within lines to emphasize dramatic relationships between words and ideas. In "Falling," for example, a stewardess's plunge from an airborne plane is graphically represented through the open form, which suggests the bizarre, unexpected, chaotic nature of her experience:

                                        As though she blew

The door down with a silent blast from her lungs   frozen   she is black
Out finding herself   with the plane nowhere and her body taking by
      the throat
The undying cry of the void[15]

Furthermore, Dickey's language here, as throughout his work, creates a dramatic tension between the stewardess's predicament and the poet's tone. For example, in "she is black / Out finding herself," the reader at first might assume that the stewardess is a black woman or that she has been frozen black or

UNDERSTANDING JAMES DICKEY

that she has blacked out. Finally the reader realizes the poet's intention—to show that she is now in the blackness of night, like the airplane, although the plane is now nowhere in sight. "Falling" also illustrates how Dickey plunges the reader immediately into the poem's action. Its verbal forms—particularly the present participles—provide a sense of immediacy, and the reader falls through the darkness alongside the stewardess, discovering what she discovers as she falls.

Another development in Dickey's later poetic technique has been what he labels "associational imagery."[16] Although he offers no definition of the term, he declares that "Pine" employs this sort of imagery. An examination of the work's first lines may reveal how the imagery works:

> Low-cloudly it whistles, changing heads
> On you. How hard to hold and shape head-round.
> So any hard hold
> Now loses; form breathes near. Close to forest-form
> By ear, so landscape is eyelessly
> Sighing through needle-eyes.[17]

Here Dickey describes the wind in terms of a series of breath images encompassing clouds ("Low-cloudly it whistles"), natural forms ("form breathes near. Close to forest-form / By ear"), and the panorama of nature ("so landscape is eyelessly / Sighing"). The imagery lies in verb and verbal forms, and thus seems more fluid—if also less concrete and comprehensible—than traditional forms. Associational imagery, which makes considerable demands on the reader, also operates in the late work *Puella*. There it becomes part of a highly lyrical language that tends as well to lessen the poet's emphasis on narrative, on action.

Throughout his work James Dickey dramatizes a Self that constantly evolves, constantly explores what he calls that "strong relationship between what you write and how you live. . . . I have never been able to disassociate the poem from the poet, and I hope I never will. I really don't believe in Eliot's theory of autotelic art, in which the poem has nothing to do with the man who wrote it. . . . I think they're absolutely incapable of being disassociated from each other."[18] What Dickey has experienced as a man becomes the raw material for his art. His surviving the war has greatly affected how he lives his life and re-creates it in his art. As he states in "The Poet Turns on Himself," "Underlying everything he [the poet] writes is the dual sense of being glad to be alive to write that particular poem and of outrage at the possibility of the loss of all things that have meant much to him—outrage that these personal, valuable things could ever be definitively lost for anyone."[19] And it is with this mixture of joy and outrage that Dickey explores the world he creates through his work.

Notes

1. George Garrett, "Snapshot," *The Writer's Voice: Conversations with Contemporary Writers*, ed. Garrett (New York: Morrow, 1973) 229.

2. Dickey, "The Poet Turns on Himself," *Babel to Byzantium: Poets and Poetry Now* (New York: Farrar, Straus, and Giroux, 1968) 292.

INTO THE STONE AND *DROWNING WITH OTHERS*

confrontation with it or, more accurately, with the Self that death has marked. This confrontation—or the "sustained questioning" that produces "the psychology of the survivor" with its attendant "guilt," as Lifton describes it[2]—may seem most appropriate to the war poetry; yet it also clearly underlies the poet's treatment of family, love, and nature in the collection.

One of Dickey's best-known war poems, "The Performance,"[3] uses three central characters—Donald Armstrong, a Japanese executioner, and the work's narrator—to illustrate different responses to death. Armstrong, a downed flyer, performs a series of startling gymnastic tricks moments before he is beheaded by his captors; doing "All things in this life that he could," he conveys a "strange joy" through his final defiant gesture against death. The Japanese "headsman," moved by Armstrong's display, breaks down in "a blaze of tears," but then completes the performance the two are engaged in by beheading the American with a two-handed sword. Both play their roles, as they must, in death's drama, but each gives more than might be expected.

The third character—the narrator—has not witnessed the performance, but must instead re-create it through his imagination. Learning "how he died," the speaker invests Armstrong with "kingly" attributes—courage, grace, composure— and he feels pride in his friend's triumphant stance against death. Yet there is also the suggestion that the narrator may not regard himself as quite equal to his friend or to the magnitude of his performance:

UNDERSTANDING JAMES DICKEY

> The last time I saw Donald Armstrong
>
> . . . .
> I let my shovel fall, and put that hand
> Above my eyes, and moved some way to one side
> That his body might pass through the sun.

While Armstrong walks on his hands, the speaker is digging. While Armstrong performs in the blazing sun, the speaker must move to one side and shield his eyes from the sun; and he repeats the hand-to-forehead gesture when he begins his imaginative re-creation of events. Clearly the narrator is awed by the flyer's courage and anguished by his loss. The imagery may also imply the speaker's sense that Armstrong, a bona fide hero, has died better than the speaker might have, that Armstrong may have died, in fact, in his place. This, Lifton asserts, is a common feeling in combat survivors,[4] a feeling that induces guilt and a very real ambivalence about the self.

The same ambivalence exists in "The Jewel,"[5] a poem portraying the aftereffects, years later, of involvement in war. Peacefully camping with his sons, the middle-aged narrator becomes "A man doubled strangely in time." The tent, the night, the reflection in his coffee cup of "a smile I was issued" during the war draw him back into his experiences as a member of a night bomber crew years before. "Forgetting I am alive," he imaginatively reenters the "great, stressed jewel," his plane, and switches on "A strong, poor diamond of light" that shines "like the meaning of war." In this setting he must remain detached, must not question what he is doing, must be one who "Has taken his own vow of silence / *Alone, in late night.*"

INTO THE STONE AND *DROWNING* *WITH OTHERS*

In the poem's last stanza, however, the speaker returns to present time and voices very real questions:

> Truly, do I live? Or shall I die, at last,
> Of waiting? Why should the fear grow loud
> With the years, of being the first to give in
> To the matched, priceless glow of the engines,
> *Alone, in late night?*

He fears being a victim of war's hold on him—of loving too much its drama and jewel-like beauty. Equally important, he fears that his concerns about dying and causing death in combat have carried over into his present-day, peacetime life. Even now he cannot be sure that he is truly alive, that he is not dying each moment through the violent, perplexing memories he contains. As "The Jewel" clearly suggests, war does claim its victims—either immediately on the battlefield or later, and perhaps more painfully, in the mind of the combat survivor.

The writer's concern with death and its power in the war poems reappears in his family poems of *Into the Stone*. In this volume Dickey focuses on his relationship with his older brother, Eugene, a figure with whom he wishes to connect but from whom he also desires to escape. In *Self-Interviews* the poet discusses the source of his ambivalence toward his dead brother:

I *did* have an older brother, Eugene, who died before I was born, and I *did* gather by implication and hints of family relatives that my mother, an invalid with angina pectoris, would not have dared to have another child if Gene had lived. I was the child who was born as a result of this situation. And I have always felt a sense of guilt that my birth depended on my brother's death.[6]

In "The String,"[7] the speaker re-creates for his own son the elaborate string structures that Eugene had woven while on his deathbed:

> Except when he enters my son,
> The same age as he at his death,
> I cannot bring my brother to myself.
> I do not have his memory in my life,
> Yet he is in my mind and on my hands.
> I weave the trivial string upon a light
> *Dead before I was born.*

The structures are a fragile but tenacious link between the living and the dead, between the speaker and his older brother. The narrator imagines that Eugene has woven a heavenly "city" to which he has ascended in death. He has created the perfect work of art, has "completed the maze of my fingers." Yet Eugene, who "thought like a spider," has also, of course, been caught in a web, the "maze" of death. And more importantly he has, in dying, ensnared his younger brother, who was conceived "Out of grief . . . To replace the incredible child." The speaker thus feels real ambivalence toward both Eugene and his parents. He owes his life to them and yet he cannot hope to measure up to the "incredible" brother.

Having acknowledged his link with and obligation to his brother in "The String," the narrator in "The Underground Stream"[8] attempts to connect with Eugene by sending his

INTO THE STONE AND *DROWNING WITH OTHERS*

voice and spirit down through the subterranean stream. For Dickey rivers and underground streams are important devices for joining the world of the living, the "upper, springtime world," with that of the dead, the "sill of oblivion." As the speaker sends his message to his brother, Eugene in turn tries

> To rise through a circle of stone,
> . . . .
> And claim his own grave face
> That mine might live in its place.

Both smile at the possibility of union, of exchange, but whether it is achieved remains, like the relationship of the brothers, highly ambiguous: "I lay at the edge of a well; / And then I smiled, and fell." Whether the speaker's fall is into the waters of connection or into a well of disappointed hope cannot be determined.

"The Other"[9] portrays Eugene not as an "incredible child" but instead as godlike and "king-sized," and the narrator's ambivalence seems to increase with the specter's size. As the speaker chops at a tree in an attempt to transform his own meager body into the ideal proportions enjoyed by his brother, Eugene plays a "great harp" and sings "Of the hero, withheld by its body." Through his brother's music the speaker gains an awareness of what he could become:

> Reason fell from my mind at a touch
> Of the cords, and the dead tree leapt
> From the ground, and together, and alive.
> I thought of my body to come;
> My mind burst into that green.

UNDERSTANDING JAMES DICKEY

Just as the music is able to change the chopped, dead wood into a living tree, so too can Eugene transform the speaker from a "rack-ribbed child" into a more muscular "bronze-bodied shape / . . . mixed with a god's." The physical change suggests a spiritual exchange. Yet the relationship between the two seems tinged with hostility. The narrator dramatically calls for a release from the phantom who drives and obsesses him: "My body-building angel give me rest"; and Eugene is both benign and malevolent, for he does not leave but rather remains in the tree hissing at his living brother. The relationship thus continues to cause ambivalence in the narrator.

The war and family poems of *Into the Stone* reflect the writer's mixed feelings about his own survival when so many have died; consequently his affection and admiration for friends and family are edged with anguish, with a sense of obligation. In the volume's title poem, however, Dickey asserts that love, like the creative process, can be a principal means of countering death. Sharing the dead's potential for resurrection—"Like the dead, I have newly arisen"—the speaker of "Into the Stone"[10] travels to a waiting woman to whom he gives his "heart all the way into moonlight." Once he gains such love, he asserts, "No thing that shall die as I step / May fall, or not sing of rebirth." Love seems to promise the living a transformation into a more intense, fully lived experience and to grant the dead a real opportunity for rebirth: "The dead have their chance in my body."

The sexual union between the man and the woman is paralleled to the bond between the sun and the moon. The moon,

INTO THE STONE AND *DROWNING WITH OTHERS*

the great stone in the heavens, is for Dickey often associated with love and creativity, since it gives off—as Howard Nemerov suggests—an illumination that grants the poet a unique vision of his world. Many of Dickey's speakers, Nemerov points out, are men alone in the dark of night; but their blindness is cured by the moonlight, which grants them visionary, imaginative powers.[11] When stone imagery is related to the moon, it usually announces the poet's rise beyond the world of death and loss; when it is on the earth or in water, the stone often represents the boundary separating the worlds of life and death, the boundary through which one must pass, as in "The Underground Stream."

"Into the Stone" is an unusually optimistic examination of love; normally Dickey's treatment of all aspects of what he calls the "man-made world"[12] is fraught with emotional strains and complexities: deaths of loved ones, agonizing aftereffects of war, and difficulties in achieving love. These emotional dilemmas primarily result from his speakers' struggles for meaningful survival. Yet in the nature-centered universe Dickey finds a source for genuine spiritual wholeness, at least initially.

In two closely related poems, "Sleeping Out at Easter" and "The Vegetable King," Dickey's protagonist comes to understand nature's cycle of life, death, and rebirth. Each spring he camps alone in a small grove of pines and thus leaves behind as many traces of the civilized world as possible. During the night, while in the posture of the dead, he dreams his vision of the seasons' eternal cycle of death and renewal and then returns to his family. Yet the two poems convey different conclusions.

"Sleeping Out at Easter"[13] reveals that the speaker's bed is equivalent to "the grave of the king." When he rises the next morning, as Christ did at Easter, the protagonist feels resurrected, transformed into "light": "My sight is the same as the sun's." The play on "sun" suggests that the narrator has gained the sight of the Son of God as well as nature's source of light and life. He achieves not only a union with nature, a conception of the Self as the center point around which the earth revolves, but also a perception of the creative source of life:

> . . . my right hand, buried beneath me,
> Hoveringly tingles, with grasping
> The sources of all song at the root.

When he returns home to his family, the narrator is "blazing" with the "light" and the "Word," as if he were Christ risen from the grave and adored for his power of spiritual transformation. The poet's language suggests that a holy ceremony has occurred—significantly at night in the moonlight—culminating in his passing on to his son the abilities of the prophetic seer. The tone of celebration marks this poem, like "Into the Stone," as another of the few instances of clear triumph in Dickey's work.

Using the same setting as "Sleeping Out at Easter," "The Vegetable King"[14] combines the Christian resurrection imagery with the Osiris myth, which Dickey identifies in *Self-Interviews*.[15] As the sleeping central figure dreams, he adopts the character of Osiris, whose body is dismembered and of-

INTO THE STONE AND *DROWNING WITH OTHERS*

fered as sacrifice and then rejoined to ensure the return of spring and life again. Rising from "the whole of mindless nature" to "become that man, become / As bloodless as a god," the speaker returns home and asks that his family restore his original identity:

> Mother, son, and wife
>
> Who live with me: I am in death
> And waking. Give me the looks that recall me.
> . . . .
> you have set
> These flowers upon the table, and milk for him
> Who, recurring in this body, bears you home
> Magnificent pardon, and dread, impending crime.

Yet he remains Osiris-Christ, who does bear with him pardon and crime. And since the pardon (the loving, forgiving renewal) is followed in the line by the crime (death), Dickey implies that death in fact prevails despite the powers of love. As in much of his poetry in this collection, then, the confrontation with death causes real ambivalence in the speaker.

In "Sleeping Out at Easter" and "Into the Stone," Dickey suggests that connection with a loved one or with nature can provide successful barriers against death, successful expiators of his own sense of guilt. However, in the other poems of the volume he sets forth a more complex vision, one that allows him little true repose. The latter tone also dominates the works in his next collection.

Drowning with Others further explores the process of confrontation with death or with the Self that death has marked. In this collection Dickey increasingly portrays his narrator as occupying a middle ground between the world of death (typically the underworld, although in "Armor" the place of the dead is the heavens) and the world of heightened life and vision (as in "The Owl King"). The protagonist desires to achieve union with or complete understanding of each world. But if a figure can occasionally ascend to the heightened state of the owl king, his efforts to exchange identities with the dead must be halted short of completion, for to succeed in this effort would mean destruction of the Self.

Two war poems in *Drowning with Others* dramatize speakers' efforts to discover what the dead know. In "Between Two Prisoners,"[16] Dickey portrays American flyers bound by wire in a Philippines schoolhouse and awaiting beheading. They are watched by a Japanese guard who will himself, "A year later, to the day," be hanged in Manilla. Between the condemned—American and Japanese—passes a language, a message, "That the unbound, who walk, cannot know." The speaker, a survivor, dares not interpret this "foreign tongue," as it belongs only to the realm of the dead and contains all the secrets of death—"All things that cannot be said" to or by the living.

In contrast, the speaker in "The Island"[17] tries to penetrate the secrets of the war dead, to clasp "every thought in my head / That bloomed from the magical dead." He accomplishes his goal by burying the bodies of the dead, erecting wooden crosses above their graves, and setting up a picket fence around the plot. He clearly identifies with the dead:

INTO THE STONE AND DROWNING WITH OTHERS

> Each wooden body, I took
> In my arms and singingly shook
> With its being, which stood for my own
> More and more, as I laid it down.

He then undertakes an elaborate funeral ceremony to free himself from death: he salutes the graves "by their rank" and dances "unimagined and free." Yet he has, the poem suggests, gone too far; for the troopship has left him on the island, and he is isolated with the dead; he becomes himself an island, physically and emotionally a captive to each dead man who "nourishes" him.

Just as the war dead intensify their emotional hold on Dickey's protagonist in "The Island" and pull him downward into their underworld, so too does a spirit of death in "Armor"[18] encompass him, "Like a brother whose features I knew." The protagonist dons a protective suit of armor to be worn

> Not into the rattling of battle,
>
> But into a silence where nothing
> Threatens but Place itself.

Because this threatening site ironically has an idyllic appearance, it makes the protagonist vulnerable to the "strange, crowned / Motionless sunlight of Heaven," where his dead brother waits for him "Like a hanged man waiting in Heaven." The armor, like the beautiful setting, does not offer protection from such sunlight; rather, it seems to encourage the speaker's desires to yield to the spiritual pull of the dead.

Unable to escape from such light or such introspection while dressed in his armor, he removes it. Returning home to sleep, he rests with his hands on his chest—"like the dead on my heart"—and in a fevered dream envisions his brother turning slowly "Under the strange, perfect branches" of a tree. The speaker longs to dress "at last / In the gold of my waiting brother." Yet he knows that he will not be able to recognize either his brother or his own "dazed, eternal" face until he touches the eternal armor in which his brother is dressed and

> Until I have let the still sun
> Down into the stare of the eyepiece
> And raised its bird's beak to confront
> What man is within to live with me
> When I begin living forever.

Ironically, to live forever is to die, and the speaker is not yet ready to follow his confrontation with death to its logical conclusion.

The protagonist is pulled by the dead in two directions—downward into the underworld and upward into the heavens. Even while wearing armor he cannot shield himself from the pervasiveness of the dead's hold on him. The tree as part of the "Place" in which the two brothers gain access to each other becomes a more prominent conduit between the living and the dead in yet another family poem.

"In the Tree House at Night"[19] dramatizes the poet's attempt to find a balance between the living and the dead. A mid-station between earth and sky, the tree house becomes an important natural setting for the speaker's communion with

his one dead and his one living brother. Following the directions of their dead brother that "we must ascend" to this location, they build a version of Jacob's ladder that takes them
halfway to heaven. And inside this house

> We lie here like angels in bodies,
> My brothers and I, one dead,
> The other asleep from much living.

The living brothers climb their tree house and, adopting the
supine position of the dead, cover themselves with a blanket
"as solid as stone," as if buried in the earth. The speaker's dead
brother then travels up the tree's roots extending into the lower
world of the dead and joins the sleeping, living brothers. Once
this connection is made between the dead and the living,
nature—the "green household" outside their house—comes
alive, and "One bird uncontrollably cries" in a burst of joy, reflecting the love shared by the brothers.

However, almost simultaneously the narrator raises key
questions about his experience, questions reminiscent of those
voiced in "The Jewel."

> The wind changes round, and I stir
> Within another's life. Whose life?
> Who is dead? Whose presence is living?
> When may I fall strangely to earth,
>
> Who am nailed to this branch by a spirit?

These questions, which strike at the heart of the protagonist's
uncertainty about his relationship with the living and the

dead, cannot be answered. Yet he envisions himself as a survivor nailed to a tree "by a spirit." The earlier joyful tone is undercut by the dead brother's capacity to inflict an agonizing spiritual wound on the speaker, who is caught between a deep longing to commune with his dead brother and a necessary turning away from him. To preserve his own life he must maintain the boundary or mid-point between the living and the dead. The tree house provides this mid-point, where he can move "at the heart of the world." He therefore can remain alive, although he will still suffer an acute consciousness of the dead.

The emotional imprisonment dramatized in the war and family poems in *Drowning with Others* reappears in a kind of love poem, "In the Lupanar at Pompeii."[20] While the narrator sits alone examining the ancient wall drawings of sexual activities, he feels that he "could be in prison, or dead, / Cast down for my sins in a cell." The prison images suggest not only punishment for sins of the flesh but also the emptiness of humans—like the prostitutes once living in this now empty building—who feel no genuine love or passion. Yet the artificiality of these drawings ironically elicits a genuine surge of desire within the protagonist:

> I think of the marvel of lust
> Which can always, at any moment,
> Become more than it believed,
> And almost always is less:
> I think of its possible passing
> Beyond, into tender awareness,
> Into helplessness, weeping, and death.

INTO THE STONE AND *DROWNING* *WITH OTHERS*

Lust may offer a complete though momentary awakening of passion. It is in this sense liberating. When, however, it is elevated to love, it takes on all the complexities of other human experiences. It provides a fulfilling but also emotionally threatening relationship for the speaker.

His protagonists' confrontations with the dead and with the potential for death within themselves often illustrate the poet's feeling of obligation to those who have died, seemingly in his place. The guilt that thereby arises also appears in figures who are not intended directly to represent the poet but instead mankind at large. "The Lifeguard"[21] dramatizes a predicament in some ways analogous to that in "The Island." However, this protagonist's service for the dead results not from a vague sense of his own responsibility for the dead, but from a certain one.

The lifeguard fails in his duties when a small boy in his care drowns. To assuage his agonizing guilt the man returns to the lake at night and repeatedly dives in hope of recovering the boy's body. The lifeguard's isolation heightens his despair as he searches through the opaque, dark water with its surface like stone separating the living from the dead. Since the only light by which the guard can see is moonlight, the would-be rescuer pleads for vision to see beyond life into the underworld of the dead. He calls for the child, and

> the child's
> Voice answers through blinding water.
> Patiently, slowly,
>
> He rises, . . .

The man's guilt makes him believe that he can perform the impossible, that he can bring the child back to life and thus become "The savior of one / Who has already died in my care." Yet the imagery—the apparent solidity of the dark water through which the lifeguard gropes with "fingertips turned into stone"—suggests that this location can support only death. As he returns to shore, his anguished, imaginative vision fails him, for the child he "hold[s]" in his arms is only "a child / Of water, water, water," an image that forever marks the guilt of death on his hands.

The lifeguard's attempt to save a child from death illustrates a predicament that often appears in Dickey's work: a father (or father figure) searches for his child who is lost, alone, and often blind. The father's possible or actual loss produces in him devastating guilt. The lifeguard's failure is countered in "The Owl King"[22] by a successful search for and rescue of a child. Equally as important, "The Owl King" dramatizes a force opposing the downward pull of death. In several poems of this volume the poet reveals that man has the capacity to rise beyond his earthly station to kingship. "Drowning with Others," for example, features a man who unhitches his shoulders so that they can evolve into wings. Yet, as "Armor" shows, if a man ascends too high, he runs the risk of joining the spirits of the dead in the heavens, thereby losing his life through such a heightened connection. Instead, he must move only as high as that mid-point between earth and sky, as in "In the Tree House at Night," or as high as the owl's perch, as in "The Owl King." From these vantage points one can learn to

INTO THE STONE AND *DROWNING WITH OTHERS*

see the world with a special vision that encompasses both life and death.

"The Owl King" is divided into three sections recording the voices of three different speakers: "The Call" briefly portrays the father searching at night for his lost blind son; "The Owl King" records the meditations of the wild royal creature; and "The Blind Child's Story," the poem's longest section, recounts the boy's growing awareness of how to perceive his world. The father, feeling "the deep dead turn / My blind child round toward my calling," is uncertain whether the dead intend to claim the boy as their own or to lead him to safety. Ironically, the father is the one who is truly lost and blind in the forest, for in the owl's dark domain the man relies upon the wrong kind of vision, the wrong kind of light with which to see. In contrast, the owl has the natural ability to perceive the world "as . . . it must be" with his "blazing, invented eyes." In turn, he teaches the blind child, who sits with him high in an oak tree, how truly to see with vision gained from moonlight, again an image of the imagination. Listening to his father's desperate call, the child notes:

> I learn from the master of sight
> What to do when the sun is dead,
> How to make the great darkness work
> As it wants of itself to work.

The death of the sun suggests the fulfillment of the father's worst fear, the loss of his son to a "great darkness," the world of the dead. However, the boy safely returns to his human father, after having learned from his spiritual father, the owl, to see "as the owl king sees, / By going deeper than darkness." He consequently assumes the power of the artist, the power to employ the eyes of invention to confront the darkness of this world and of the world of the dead.

The lesson nature teaches the child is also what the poet's protagonist achieves, as an artist figure, when he ventures alone into the darkness of nature. The speaker of "In the Mountain Tent"[23] feels the "profound, unspeakable law" of nature when he connects with "the minds of animals." Such a union gives him the "dark, like light, out of Heaven," a light similar to that found in "Armor," from which the protagonist must finally withdraw to save his own life. Yet this light of "In the Mountain Tent" provides the protagonist with an awareness of what the true poem should encompass:

> I am there like the dead, or the beast
> Itself, which thinks of a poem—
> Green, plausible, living, and holy—
>
> . . . .
>
> The sustained intake of all breath
> Before the first word of the Bible.

Once he learns to speak with the "God-silenced tongue of the beasts," he is able to "rise from the dead" into the primordial silence before the first word of nature's creation.

When the protagonist exchanges identity with animals hunting or being hunted—those involved in a mortal struggle—his process of creation depends on his active participation in the hunt, as "A Dog Sleeping on my Feet"[24] reveals. The dog, who dreams of chasing a fox through the forest, communicates his vision through the numbed or "killed" legs of the writer on whose feet he sleeps; in turn, the man enters the dog's dream, where he runs with the creature. This exchange between man and animal allows the artist a firsthand insight into nature's hunter-hunted relationship, and the poem begins to "move" on the page as if writing itself without the aid of reason. Just as participating in the hunt poses a possible risk for the fox, surrendering himself to this method of creating his poem can threaten the life and identity of the speaker. When his dream is concluded, he therefore must reassemble himself into human form, as he has done in "Sleeping Out at Easter" and "The Vegetable King." With the completion of the hunt and the successful finish of the poem, the protagonist has gained a vital insight into his process of creativity, a process that suggests as well a means for his moving beyond the prison of death and ascending toward his own kingship.

Yet if the protagonist ascends too high into the animals' heaven, he finds an eternal cycle of death. In nature's perfected version of the predator-prey relationship, "The Heaven of Animals,"[25] each animal kills or is killed "In a sovereign floating of joy." After each kill the animals repeat their performance—without concern, without remorse—forever in the "cycle's center" of a savage, balanced order. Clearly, man does not and cannot attain such a heaven, for in his world the relationship between killed and killer, dead and living, is filled with ambiguity. Man is plagued by a mind that remembers and a heart that anguishes: he cannot enter man's heaven unless he wishes to lose his life; he cannot move to nature's heaven, for he is not psychologically equipped to participate in the unthinking, remorseless life-and-death cycle.

Man's attempts to ascend into kingship, then, must be contained in both man's and nature's worlds. The dead wait for him in both heavens—man's and nature's—as well as in the underworld. His attempts to confront the dead lead him to a mid-point between these extremes; yet it is a suspended existence that seems to provide only a momentary, rather precarious barrier against the forces of death.

Notes

1. *Babel to Byzantium* 104.
2. Lifton, *Home from the War* 388–90.
3. *Into the Stone* 59–60; *Poems 1957–1967* 30–31.
4. Lifton 106.
5. *Into the Stone* 57–58; *Poems 1957–1967* 28–29.
6. *Self-Interviews* 88–89.
7. *Into the Stone* 45–46; *Poems 1957–1967* 21–22.
8. *Into the Stone* 43–44; *Poems 1957–1967* 19–20.
9. *Into the Stone* 72–74; *Poems 1957–1967* 34–36.
10. *Into the Stone* 89–90; *Poems 1957–1967* 47–48.
11. Howard Nemerov, "Poems of Darkness and a Specialized Light," *Sewanee Review* 71 (Winter 1963) 99–104.
12. *Self-Interviews* 67.
13. *Into the Stone* 37–38; *Poems 1957–1967* 17–18.
14. *Into the Stone* 49–51; *Poems 1957–1967* 23–25.
15. *Self-Interviews* 85.
16. *Drowning with Others* (Middletown, CT: Wesleyan University Press, 1962) 43–44; *Poems 1957–1967* 78–80.

INTO THE STONE AND *DROWNING WITH OTHERS*

17. *Drowning with Others* 53–54; not reprinted in *Poems 1957–1967*.
18. *Drowning with Others* 45–46; *Poems 1957–1967* 81–82.
19. *Drowning with Others* 26–27; *Poems 1957–1967* 66–67.
20. *Drowning with Others* 47–48; *Poems 1957–1967* 83–84.
21. *Drowning with Others* 11–12; *Poems 1957–1967* 51–52.
22. *Drowning with Others* 32–40; *Poems 1957–1967* 70–77.
23. *Drowning with Others* 95–96; *Poems 1957–1967* 109–10.
24. *Drowning with Others* 15–16; *Poems 1957–1967* 55–56.
25. *Drowning with Others* 19–20; *Poems 1957–1967* 59–60.

CHAPTER THREE

Helmets

T he title of Dickey's third volume focuses on a device that advances his "reordering" of perceptions about the dead, particularly about those who died in the war. Lifton declares that reordering includes "the breaking down of some of the character armor, the long-standing defenses and maneuvers around numbed guilt."[1] Through the use of a variety of head and body adornments—helmets—the poet is able to reevaluate his responsibilities toward those he feels have died in order that he might live. As Richard Howard points out, the word *helmet* "derives from two old verbs for protecting and concealing."[2] Joseph Shipley suggests further implications for *helmet:* "There is an early Eng. verb, *hele,* to cover, to hide; and from this source comes the final hiding-place, *hell.* This was at first used of the abode of the dead, the underworld (which contained both the Elysian Fields of the blessed and Tartarus for the accursed); but its use to translate Gr. *gehenna,* in the New Testament, turned it into a haunt of the fiends and the devils, horrid hell."[3]

HELMETS

The helmet used for protection and concealment from forces that can endanger the poet may seem a surprising symbol for a writer who scorns life reduced to half-passions and indirect confrontations. Dickey believes strongly in an "energized" life that moves a man to the edge of danger to gain a passionate consequence in his life. Yet if he strives for a great consequence, he also risks great failure—that of moving too close to death. Consequently, he needs a device that can shield and perhaps save him.

But the symbol of the helmet is not limited only to protection and concealment. When he puts on a variety of head and body coverings, the poet also achieves a changed perspective through his exchange of identity with the former owner or wearer of the helmet. Thus, the helmet grants him a means of communication, usually with the dead. At times the perspective he gains is a terrifying one, while at other moments it is lyrical, even glorious, thus reflecting the differences between the Elysian Fields of the blessed and Tartarus, the place of the accursed in the world of the dead. *Helmets* dramatizes important variations on the image and theme of the helmet, which becomes an organizing symbol for the entire volume of poems.

Three war poems in this volume plot the poet's efforts to communicate with the dead. "Horses and Prisoners," like "The Performance" and "Between Two Prisoners" in the earlier volumes, treats the subject of war's captives; in "The Driver" the speaker attempts a personal connection with one who has died in the war; and, finally, in "Drinking from a Helmet" the poet successfully achieves his vision of what the dead know.

Rather than re-creating possible events in his imagination, as do the speakers in "The Performance" and "Between Two Prisoners," the protagonist in " Horses and Prisoners"[4] directly observes men as prisoners and thereby puts himself near the center of his drama. On a racetrack where the narrator "sat at the finish line / At the end of the war / Knowing that I would live," he watches the grisly process of life being "Sustained by the death of beasts," as the prisoners of war tear at the raw flesh of horses to escape starvation. Knowing that he will live beyond the war leads the protagonist to believe that he can triumph over death—"When death moves close / In the night, I think I can kill it"—a conviction that results in part from his sharing the prisoners' predicament and their clear desire for life.

While "Horses and Prisoners" establishes his belief that he can triumph over death, "The Driver"[5] chronicles a test of his conviction that he can defeat death and learn what the dead feel and think. Swimming and singing in the sea, the protagonist celebrates the war's end and his "new thought of peace." Beneath him, however, he sees a landing craft that was destroyed while trying to take the beach. He sinks to the buried craft's seat and tries to adopt the former driver's perspective by imitating the "burning stare" of the dead man. The protagonist, however, comes close to drowning, for he stays too long under water; he must

> . . . leap at last for the sky
> Very nearly too late, where another

> Leapt and could not break into
> His breath, . . .

The closest the narrator can come to comprehending the dead is through his reenactment of the dead man's final realization:

> "I become pure spirit," I tried
> To say, . . .
> But I was becoming no more
> Than haunted, for to be so
> Is to sink out of sight, and to lose
> The power of speech in the presence
> Of the dead, . . .

H. L. Weatherby states that "to be haunted is to take upon oneself the condition of the dead, to be possessed by the dead, and that is what the swimmer does."[6]

To communicate with the dead the speaker must not lose his "power of speech"; but the sea, the "lyrical skin" dividing "death and life," defeats the protagonist's efforts to connect with the dead. Being transparent, the sea should reveal its secrets of death and life, but instead it maintains the boundary between the dead and the living by not allowing the speaker to pierce its "skin." His close proximity to, but eventual failure in, joining the dead increases his anxieties about his obligations to the dead.

Though it defeats his attempts at communication in "The Driver," water becomes the medium for the speaker's successful comprehension of death in the third war poem in this volume. In "Drinking from a Helmet"[7] the protagonist does cross the boundary separating life and death through a visionary exchange of identity with a dead soldier. This transformation provides a moment of communication with the dead and the poet's long-sought-after connection with death in order to clarify his own life, his own survival. The narrator in this poem undergoes a transformation that involves moving from his own fearful isolation while surrounded by death, to an understanding of the dead soldier from whose helmet he drinks, and finally to a more universal vision of death.

"Drinking from a Helmet" contains 19 stanzas organized into four movements. The first three sections consist of five stanzas each, while the fourth contains four. The first movement (stanzas 1 through 5) establishes the seventeen-year-old speaker's resignation to his own death; he is "tired of waiting / For my foxhole to turn in the earth / On its side or its back for a grave." Noting the cemetery that keeps pace with the advance of his comrades in combat, he waits for death while in the midst of this stark contrast of life and death on the battlefield. When a water truck appears, the protagonist grabs a dead man's helmet from which to drink, for he is afraid to remove his own, to abandon the special properties of protection the helmet offers. Before the speaker drinks from the borrowed helmet, however, the poem moves to a description of the protagonist's first beard, which signals the beginning of his rite of passage from youth to manhood.

The second movement of the poem (stanzas 6 through 10) starts with the speaker's initial drink of water from the borrowed helmet.

HELMETS

> I drank, with the timing of rust.
> A vast military wedding
> Somewhere advanced one step.

The ceremony suggests the marriage of life and death; and drinking, the protagonist is struck by a series of surrealistic, whirling scenes reflected in the helmet: "equipment drifting in light," "Grass pouring down from the sun," and "Bright circles . . . inward and outward" give him a sense that he is "trembling forward through something / Just born of me." What is "born" within him is a realization that he is connected to the dead as well as to the living, primarily because of the helmet. This particular apparel has been created in mythic circumstances:

> . . . in a harvest of sparks,
> The helmet leapt from the furnace
> And clamped itself
> On the heads of a billion men.

The "furnace" and "sparks" that issue from the borrowed helmet suggest the world of hell, as well as the hell of combat. Its attachment to "a billion men" universally connects the living with the dead as much as it joins the speaker with the individual dead soldier. Such a vision causes the protagonist to feel almost overcome: "I swayed, as if kissed in the brain."

As he undergoes the transformation from isolated soldier to one who connects with a dead man, the speaker assumes a new character inside him in the poem's third movement (stanzas 11 through 15):

> I stood as though I possessed
> A cool, trembling man
> Exactly my size, swallowed whole.

Symbolically, that is precisely what occurs, for while still maintaining his own separate identity, he gains the legacy of the dead:

> The dead cannot rise up,
> But their last thought hovers somewhere
> For whoever finds it.

When he puts on the borrowed helmet, the warm water runs over his face and allows the speaker to acquire this dead man's last thought. Now the water functions as a kind of holy water which baptizes the speaker into a new life and communion with the dead.

The dead man's final thought—a serene scene of two brothers bicycling through the California redwoods—gives the protagonist a vision of peace beyond the context of war, a tranquil heaven which contrasts to his hell on the battlefield. Because the speaker experiences both the living hell of combat and the peaceful calm of death, his exchange or transformation is at once liberating and damning. He learns indeed what the dead feel and think; at the same time, the momentary last thought of the dead man does not offer final peace for him, especially when he returns to the realities of war. The speaker decides that after the war he will find the dead man's brother "And tell him I was the man," an echo of Dickey's quotation of Whitman in "The Self as Agent": " 'I was the man, I suffer'd,

HELMETS

I was there.' "[8] As Lifton reveals, "witnessing" is a part of
psychological "reordering": "Bearing witness implies being
present to share pain and wisdom, and to take on the responsibility to 'tell the story' afterward."[9]

In "Drinking from a Helmet," the helmet is used not only
for protection and concealment but also for communion with
the dead; the latter function dominates in "Approaching Prayer,"[10] as the protagonist attempts prayer to his father, through
whose house he wanders

> Looking for things to put on
> Or to strip myself of
> So that I can fall to my knees
> And produce a word I can't say
> Until all my reason is slain.

He puts on his father's gray sweater, which imitates the older
man's "gray body hair," his father's gamecock spurs, and the
head of the boar the protagonist killed in a hunt that gave him
his own "best and stillest moment." Once the speaker slips his
own head inside the "hollow hog's head," the poem instantly
re-creates the night of the hunt and death of the boar. The father's garments and the boar's head, variations on the helmet
image, provide the speaker means of exchanging his character
with that of the animal, an exchange further reflected by the
alternating points of view between hunter and hunted.

The boar stands in mid-stream—again associating water
with death, as in the underground stream imagery—and
watches the man draw his bow. Though the speaker labels his
thoughts as "irrelevancies one thinks of / When trying to

pray," these hunting scenes are in fact the heart of his prayer. As he motionlessly aims the arrow at the boar, the protagonist sees

> Beasts, angels
>
> . . . .
> The moon and the stars do not move
>
> . . . .
> The planets attune all their orbits.

He achieves his still moment, his prayer, and utters the word "Yes." This personal and universal affirmation is his prayer uttered at the moment of the boar's death. He has discovered the right relationship with nature—as a hunter with the hunted; once this brief moment occurs, man, beast, and the heavens are properly aligned.

But though his prayer puts him in accord with nature, the speaker goes too far; he crosses over the boundary separating life and death:

> I have said something else
>
> . . . .
> The universe is creaking like boards
> Thumping with heartbeats
> And bonebeats
>
> . . . .
> My father is pale on my body.

The "something" that goes through him is a shaft of light duplicating the arrow that kills the boar; now the protagonist has moved from merely visualizing the boar's death to feeling death within himself, causing in turn his universe to go awry.

HELMETS

Through the boar's viewpoint the protagonist has gained a firsthand, horrifying realization of his own mortality.

Shaken by this knowledge, the speaker, eager to stop this vision and resume his own identity, removes his father's garments and the boar's head. He determines that he will "never come back" to this place of his father. He hopes he has gained the answer to "what questions men asked / In Heaven's tongue." What he has in fact discovered is a knowledge of the wild god of nature, a premonition of his own mortality, and an understanding of the difference between life and death. In crossing over the boundary between the two worlds, the speaker has risked losing his own identity, his own life; he has "approached" prayer—a complete surrender to death—but now he realizes that he must not come this close to the boundary again.

Dickey's protagonists who wear some form of helmet receive knowledge about, as well as gain protection for, their lives. Those figures, however, who do not assume helmets suffer the world's battering physically or spiritually. Such social or public figures as "The Scarred Girl," "The Poisoned Man," "Bums, On Waking," and "A Folk Singer of the Thirties" illustrate what Norman Friedman calls the "wound-motif" in Dickey's work.[11]

A girl's face crashes through a car windshield in "The Scarred Girl,"[12] and although she develops an inner beauty that replaces her former outer beauty, she must confront a world that will see the scars first and her inner loveliness later, if at all. The other figures in the social poems in this volume suffer similar downfalls: "The Poisoned Man"[13] is bitten by a rattlesnake; "Bums, On Waking" [14] are social outcasts; and "A Folk Singer of the Thirties"[15] is mutilated, nailed to a railroad car. The symbolic settings of the hospital and the cemetery become prominent locations for these and comparable figures. But perhaps the most important brutalization to the body and the spirit of these unprotected figures is that they are finally isolated and solitary, contending with their personal griefs alone. They are without means of protection from the world or connection to those who might provide comfort.

One means of connecting with others seemingly denied these wounded figures is the love relationship. In *Helmets* Dickey dramatizes love with a comic touch that nonetheless does not conceal the dangerous possibilities that could occur. Those who love risk themselves in order to enjoy a proportionate opportunity for emotional consequence. "Cherrylog Road"[16] celebrates a young protagonist's sexual encounter with Doris Holbrook in an automobile junkyard despite the violent threats of the girl's overly protective, suspicious father. The poem's comic tone—a shield of comedy—protects both characters from taking their lovemaking too seriously as well as conceals from them the actual danger that could occur later on.

Drawing body heat from the bootleggers' junked cars blistering in the sun, the narrator waits for Doris to meet him after she escapes from her father. The junkyard is filled with lifeless cars, insects, and snakes, dead or asleep in the hot sun. But when they hear Doris tapping a wrench to announce her arrival, the speaker and the junkyard creatures stir with ex-

citement and life. As the young couple make love in the back
seat of a car, a comic parallel is drawn between the energetic
lovers and the junkyard coming to life around them:

> I held her and held her and held her,
> Convoyed at terrific speed
> By the stalled, dreaming traffic around us,
> So the blacksnake, stiff
> With inaction, curved back
> Into life, and hunted the mouse
>
> With deadly overexcitement, . . .

The girl's dangerous father threatens her with a beating and
the boy with a shotgun blast should he ever find them together; instead of impeding their lovemaking, the danger posed
by Holbrook heightens their passion. Rather than guilt and remorse, the young protagonist is filled with jubilation and
power, is "Wild to be wreckage forever." He feels what the
speaker in "In the Lupanar at Pompeii" knows: that "lust / can
always, at any moment, / Become more than it believed."

Helmets begins with a series of nature poems about animals—domesticated, fenced in, led to stalls, yet keeping alive
their dreams of distant wildness. They are animals so protected
by man and concealed within domesticity that they can only
vaguely recall what they and their kind once enjoyed. This series of poems—including "The Dusk of Horses"[17] and "Fence
Wire"[18]—about domesticated animals who harbor their dreams
of the wilds culminates in "Chenille,"[19] a poem focusing on ex-
otic animals of the imagination reproduced in a quilt:

> Red whales and unicorns,
> Winged elephants, crowned ants:
>
> Beasts that cannot be thought of
> By the wholly sane.

If these are creations of the not "wholly sane," then the grandmother who devised them is afflicted with the same holy madness as the poet. Wrapped in these decorated quilts, the protagonist keeps winter's cold from him as he exists in "An inspired outline of myself." Dickey implies that the madness of the artist is comparable to the wildness of nature. When such madness or wildness is missing, men and animals are both reduced, and the poet—the artist—stands in vital opposition to such reduction. "Chenille" and the two poems leading up to it provide an extended metaphor for the nature poems in this volume; they indicate how the truly alive deny themselves complete protection and concealment in order to live as fully as possible.

The poet achieves such a heightened experience in nature when he engages animals as a predator looking for prey. In "Springer Mountain"[20] the speaker, a hunter, pursues and eventually finds a deer. Heavily clothed, the narrator wears four sweaters and a wool hood, and in addition his breath takes "shape on the air / Like a white helmet." The helmet imagery in this poem helps the hunter gain a moment of connection with the deer; they stop and look at each other as if transfixed. But, as in the poems about domesticated animals,

HELMETS

the narrator desires to live beyond his ordinary life as wildly and as completely as possible.

While the deer stands unafraid before him, the protagonist removes all of his clothes—all of his protection and concealment—presenting himself to the animal and to nature in a state of physical and spiritual nakedness. With the removal of his last garment "The world catches fire," signaling a successful exchange between man and animal. The man dreams of being the deer, while the deer recognizes the other as an ideal representative of his human world. Once this spiritual bond is achieved between the two, the man dances before the deer, and then they run through the forest together;

> He is moving. I am with him
>
> . . . .
> My brain dazed and pointed with trying
> To grow horns, glad that it cannot,
> For a few steps deep in the dance
> Of what I most am and should be,
> And can be only once in this life.

The protagonist does experience nature's wildness, yet his experience is one that cannot be sustained. His desire to remove the barriers between man and animal cannot fully take place; he returns to his clothing, noting:

> . . . I limp
> To look for my clothes in the world,

> A middle-aged, softening man
> Grinning and shaking his head
> In amazement to last him forever.

His "limp" back into his own humanness is a regretful return to the world of man. Yet, as he dresses to hunt "for the first and last time," he has discovered what few others find—a partial union with the wildness of nature—and the effect is enough to "last him forever."

Just as man uses helmets to protect and to conceal, so too does nature have its coverings: the sea hides the drowned; the ice protects the winter trout; water and vines cloak the shark and the snake. Once these coverings or boundaries separating nature and man are penetrated, the poet can either achieve a moment of ecstatic union with nature, as he does in "Springer Mountain," or discover a dark malevolence beneath nature's surface.

In "Kudzu,"[21] Dickey dramatizes a unique form of nature's variation on the helmet stage. This oriental vine, intended to benefit man by preventing soil erosion, instead becomes an encompassing, suffocating invasion from Japan upon the Georgia landscape. The snakelike vine silently conquers everything in its path:

> In Georgia, the legend says
> That you must close your windows
>
> At night to keep it out of the house.

But the most malevolent feature of the kudzu is that it serves as a mask for venomous snakes to hide beneath. The snake is a figure that appears frequently—as it does in the essay "The Enemy from Eden"[22]—as an emblem of nature's darker character. In Geoffrey Norman's *Playboy* interview Dickey comments on the inherent terror in both the snake and the shark: "I've always had a strong attraction to the *Other*—the thing that's most unlike humans and most unlike any other kind of life that is close to us like, say, a dog is. A shark is a low, brutal, terrifying, unpredictable, and successful form of life. The shark hit the evolutionary jackpot the first time around. He hasn't had to evolve at all in millions of years. He is very alien. So is a snake. Both of them are, I think, just about as far away from human characteristics and appearances as has yet been got. . . . A bee, for example, . . . does not evoke in me the same sense of fear and awe that a snake does or that a shark does."[23]

In "Kudzu" the snakes intertwine with the vines, rest their heads on the broad leaves, and grow "in earthly power / And the huge circumstance of concealment." To combat these deadly snakes farmers turn their hogs loose in the kudzu, and the hogs battle with the snakes with an "intense, subhuman" sound. Yet, only nature itself—killing frosts—can retard for a while the fast spread of these reptilelike vines. The benevolent "surface of things" that appears in "Sleeping Out at Easter" and "The Vegetable King" has gone mad in "Kudzu," for man dares not enter this landscape which conceals a seething fusion of vines and snakes. However, as if in league with such forces, the speaker feels the natural energy that drives the kudzu and the snakes flow into his arms, giving him a unique power as an artist. But this power conveys the strength of death rather than life.

Dickey finds in both nature's and man's worlds moments of great ecstasy and dark terror, instances of a heightened life and of deadly downfall. The helmet with its special properties helps connect and balance these extremes. In "The Ice Skin,"[24] Dickey presents a final version of the helmet's universality. While he is observing his newborn son, the protagonist's thoughts ironically turn to moments of death he has survived:

> All things that go deep enough
> Into rain and cold
> Take on, before they break down,
> A shining in every part.

Life shines in moments of glory before breaking down into death. The skin of ice that covers "all things" is a natural covering, or helmet, that draws these moments of life and death together.

The tree, an emblem of nonhuman life, dramatizes the initial instance of life touched by death. The tree absorbs the rain that turns to ice inside its trunk, causing the tree to explode like a cannon. Its branches hurtle into the air, like arms blown off a man in combat, cutting through electrical lines and plunging households into a darkness akin to death. There is no escape from the ice, for "this skin [is] / Always waiting in cold-enough air." The pervasive, frozen covering also penetrates into the speaker's memory where he catalogs scenes of life and death that haunt him: "aircraft, in war"; "the heated

HELMETS

death rooms / Of uncles"; "the heroic glaze / Also, in hospital waiting / Rooms" in which one sits "Like an emperor, fallen."

Recalling these scenes of death, the speaker views his "Just born, just born" son for the first time "Through the window of ice / . . . in his cage," the prison of life:

> I touched the frost of my eyebrows
> To the cold he turned to
> Blindly, but sensing a thing.
> Neither glass nor the jagged
> Helm on my forehead would melt.

Perceiving the "shining" of life within his son and himself, the narrator understands that such shining suggests the mixture of rain and cold creating the "breakdown" of life into death. However, the "frost" that appears first around his eyes eventually becomes through the years "ice light / In my eyes," indicating, ironically, not an impairment to the narrator's vision but rather the clarity with which he sees death's power within the living.

> I am still,
> And my son, doing what he was taught,
> Listening hard for a buried cannon,
> Stands also, calm as glass.

The protagonist's and his son's final stance in the face of certain, eventual death dramatically emphasizes the fragility of their calm as well as the power of life against death.

In his attempt to hold death at bay Dickey has aimed for a midpoint between the worlds of the living and the dead. For him, however, death is an active force that doggedly pursues him even as he tries to gain comprehension of it. To achieve knowledge of yet protection from death, the poet relies on the special characteristics of the helmet. Such knowledge helps him "reorder" his perceptions about his relationship to the dead to whom he feels a personal obligation. At the same time he learns that the "ice skin" of death is a powerful force and that he dare not finally cross the boundary separating the two worlds. The knowledge of death he acquires is thus both illuminating and terrifying.

Notes

1. Lifton, *Home from the War* 393.

2. Richard Howard, "On James Dickey," *Partisan Review* 33 (Summer 1966) 414–28, 479–86.

3. Joseph T. Shipley, *Dictionary of Word Origins* (New York: The Philosophical Library, 1945) 179.

4. *Helmets* (Middletown, CT: Wesleyan University Press, 1964), 84–86; *Poems 1957–1967* 171–72.

5. *Helmets* 81–83; *Poems 1957–1967* 169–70.

6. Weatherby, "The Way of Exchange in James Dickey's Poetry" 675.

7. *Helmets* 87–93; *Poems 1957–1967* 173–78.

8. *Sorties* 159.

9. Lifton 392.

10. *Helmets* 73–80; *Poems 1957–1967* 163–68.

11. Norman Friedman, "The Wesleyan Poets, II: The Formal Poets, 2," *Chicago Review* 19 (January 1966) 55–67, 72.

12. *Helmets* 36–37; *Poems 1957–1967* 138–39.

13. *Helmets* 44–45; *Poems 1957–1967* 145–46.

HELMETS

14. *Helmets* 65–57; *Poems 1957–1967* 159–60.

15. *Helmets* 48–54; *Poems 1957–1967* 149–53.

16. *Helmets* 31–35; *Poems 1957–1967* 134–37.

17. *Helmets* 9–10; *Poems 1957–1967* 113–14.

18. *Helmets* 11–12; *Poems 1957–1967* 115–16.

19. *Helmets* 15–17; *Poems 1957–1967* 119–21.

20. *Helmets* 27–30; *Poems 1957–1967* 130–33.

21. *Helmets* 38–41; *Poems 1957–1967* 140–42.

22. *Night Hurdling: Poems, Essays, Coversations, Commencements, and After-words* (Columbia, SC and Bloomfield Hills, MI.: Bruccoli Clark, 1983) 1–7.

23. Geoffrey Norman, "*Playboy* Interview: James Dickey," *Playboy* 20 (November 1973) 81–82, 86, 89, 92, 94, 212–216.

24. *Helmets* 62–64; *Poems 1957–1967* 157–58.

CHAPTER FOUR

Buckdancer's Choice

I n *Buckdancer's Choice* Dickey achieves full maturity as a poet. These are exciting poems, many of them discernibly longer, less constricted in form, more "open" than his previous works. In his essay "The Poet Turns on Himself," Dickey defines his concept of the "un-well-made" or "open" poem: "It would have none of the neatness of most of those poems we call 'works of art' but would have the capacity to involve the reader in it, in all its imperfections and impurities, rather than offering him a (supposedly) perfected and perfect work for contemplation, judgment, and evaluation."[1] The "open," or more conclusionless, poem not only creates the visual excitement of unexpected spatial arrangement upon the page but also invites psychological complexity, narrative power.

The poet in *Buckdancer's Choice* strips away the protecting and concealing masks employed in *Helmets* and openly addresses the questions haunting him throughout his work. In "The Firebombing," the war poem which begins the volume, he asks whether he should seek absolution or sentence for his

BUCKDANCER'S CHOICE

Air Force bombing activities. The speaker can find no easy answer; but that he is asking the question reveals his desire to move from self-laceration toward potential renewal. This question of absolution or sentence also underlies the writer's exploration of his other key subjects. In the family poems Dickey focuses on the mother-child relationship that has given him life but also produced a guilt about being alive. "Slave Quarters," an important social poem, probes the moral quandary generated by the master and slave love-hate relationship so much a part of Southern history. "The Fiend," one of his unique love poems, dramatizes another form of socially disapproved and yet curiously elevating passion. In nature, too, the writer illustrates, through "The Shark's Parlor," how a boy's victory over a shark creates both a moment of youthful glory and a lifelong haunting memory. Dickey directly treats, in the major works of this collection, the ambiguities caught in survivor's guilt.

The volume's first poem, "The Firebombing,"[2] dramatically reveals the difficulties the speaker has in bringing himself back to life after combat. Looking back on his actions during World War II, he realizes that he has had no choice about what he has done—firebombing was, after all, his duty; yet he also concedes that through his bombing missions he has caused horrifying deaths to innocent populations. Dickey has declared that the poem treats "a very complex state of mind, guilt at the inability to feel guilt."[3] His statement suggests at least some of the ambiguities that permeate the poem and its speaker's mind.

UNDERSTANDING JAMES DICKEY

As Dickey says of the protagonist in "The Jewel," the central figure in "The Firebombing" is a man "doubled strangely in time." Riding in the streetcars, sitting in bars, checking his well-stocked pantry, or shining flashlights on his palm trees in present-day America, he envisions his enemies' world which in the past he has helped to destroy. That the ordinary details of his present life persistently recall that other locale suggests the extent to which he is haunted by his past experiences, by questions about his own guilt or innocence in causing the deaths of Japanese civilians. To come to some answer he engages in a series of imaginative re-creations of his experience.

First he examines his own role during the war. As a pilot he became, like his plane, a kind of machine. He learned not to feel concern for his victims or to apply moral judgments to his actions; instead, he measured only how well he performed his task. He became "some technical-minded stranger with my hands" who flew artistically accomplished missions. As a pilot he had the power of life and death over others, but

> . . . when those on earth
> Die, there is not even sound;
> One is cool and enthralled in the cockpit,
> Turned blue by the power of beauty, . . .

Such detachment has allowed him to be a successful pilot and to perform his duty without remorse.

Yet because his actions now haunt him, he also feels compelled to envision the scenes of destruction that he has caused. As a pilot he had been "unable / To get down there or see / What really happened." Since he could not witness, could not

BUCKDANCER'S CHOICE

be there, he uses his imagination to portray what he could not see in actuality:

> All leashes of dogs
> Break under the first bomb, around those
> In bed, or late in the public baths: around those
> Who inch forward on their hands
> Into medicinal waters.
> Their heads come up with a roar
> Of Chicago fire:
> . . . .
> As I sail artistically over
> The resort town followed by farms,
> Singing and twisting
> All the handles in heaven   kicking
> The small cattle off their feet
> In a red costly blast
> Flinging jelly over the walls
> . . . .
> With fire of mine like a cat
>
> Holding onto another man's walls, . . .

Through these horrifying images which have held him for twenty years, he shows that "With this in the dark of the mind, / Death will not be what it should."

Finally, to get to the truth of his experience, the speaker tries to put himself in the place of his victims. He commands himself to

> Think of this   think of this
>
> I did not think of my house
> But think of my house now. . . .

As a homeowner seemingly in league with other homeowners, both American and Japanese, he wants to feel a sense of unity with his victims:

> All families lie together, though some are burned alive.
> The others try to feel
> For them. Some can, it is often said.

Yet the protagonist is not among those who can—simply and automatically—"feel" for these victims. Rather, his response is more complex.

He has been involved in the destruction of families hauntingly like his own; that he was just doing his duty does not, he knows, expiate him. Uncertain finally about the extent of his own moral responsibility, he will not attempt to simplify it, either for himself or others. Instead, he can only pose yet another question: "Absolution? Sentence? No matter; / The thing itself is in that." What Dickey suggests here is that the question of guilt or innocence is too complicated to be easily stated or resolved. If he wishes honestly to treat the question, he must acknowledge all the ambiguities it does, in fact, contain. Thus his speaker finally comes to no certain conclusion but instead continues to grope with the ambivalence implicit in his situation.

A similar emotional quandary is dramatized in "Buckdancer's Choice"[4] and "Angina," two family poems that focus on the mother-child relationship. Although the poet expresses great affection and admiration for his mother in these works, his feelings are also influenced by guilt. He realizes that he

BUCKDANCER'S CHOICE

has been born only because an older child has died and that his birth has endangered the life of his mother, a heart patient. Thus their relationship contains profound emotional ambiguities.

In the title poem Dickey's mother serves as a model of courage in the face of death. To counter her agony she whistles "The thousand variations of one song; / It is called Buckdancer's Choice." Through her music the child-speaker envisions the dying art of a black buck-and-wing dancer who flaps his elbows in a futile attempt to transform them into wings. Together these two performers merge in the child's mind as emblems of human refusal to give in to death:

> Through stratum after stratum of a tone
> Proclaiming what choices there are
> For the last dancers of their kind,
>
> For ill women and for all slaves
> Of death, and children enchanted at walls
> . . . .
>
> Not dancing but nearly risen
> Through barnlike, theatrelike houses
> On the wings of the buck and wing.

The personal, private arts of the two performers, which are caught in the three-beat anapestic lines, inspire the child, another slave of death, to pursue his own art years later.

Again, in "Angina,"[5] the speaker asserts that "when I think of love" it embodies itself in "an old woman" who "takes her appalling risks." Though doctors had warned her that to bear children would cause her death, she nonetheless has had four; to this woman "Existence is family," although "Her children and her children's children fail / In school, marriage, abstinence, business." Aware of her agony, the speaker stands at her bedside and hears death "saying slowly / to itself."

> I must be still and not worry,
> Not worry, not worry, to hold
> My peace, my poor place, my own.

Here the voice of death and that of the son fuse. Measured against the woman's courage, death does indeed hold a "poor place"; so too does the grown child who is conscious that he, like his siblings, has imperiled his mother's life, has caused her enormous disappointments. He thus feels a mixture of love and guilt in his relationship with her, an ambiguity that he cannot resolve but must explore.

Dickey's honesty in facing emotional truths about himself extends as well to the larger social context. Although he feels strong affection for the South, he acknowledges the guilt implicit in his region's history. In "Slave Quarters,"[6] Dickey records a contemporary white Southerner's responses to his ancestors' sexual domination of black slave women. In many respects "Slave Quarters" is about a special kind of love, but one that accommodates an active indifference which is a form of hate as well. The sexual encounters between slave owner and slave are always described as "love" in the poem, yet the owner's attitude suggests his arrogance, his complete freedom to take possession whenever he chooses and then to feel no sense of obligation or concern afterward.

BUCKDANCER'S CHOICE

Like the protagonist of "The Firebombing," Dickey's speaker is a man who bridges the present and the past, fusing the two periods in his own imagination. His dilemma, as a contemporary Southerner, involves how to acknowledge his own place within the legacy he knows was wrong:

> How take on the guilt
>
> Of slavers? How shudder like one who made
> Money from buying a people
> To work as ghosts
> In this blowing solitude?

Although he knows that the master-slave relationship was wrong, he also feels drawn to it and to the social system it implies.

While visiting the site of a former plantation, the speaker re-creates in his mind the life established in "the great house" of the South. In the daytime house of social order and decorum the plantation owner has led an aristocratic life. Like the protagonist in "The Firebombing" who surveys his well-stocked pantry and suburban home, the planter records his affluence: he is

> proud of his grounds,
> His dogs, his spinet
> From Savannah, his pale daughters,
> His war with the sawgrass, pushed back into
> The sea it crawled from.

His taming of the wilderness into a fruitful, cultivated environment sparks the contemporary Southerner's pride. But only the plantation dogs decipher what is true of both the owner and the speaker, "what I totally am"—a creature of lust and sexual power. In one sense the slave master has the same kind of power over others' lives that the pilot does in "The Firebombing."

At night, in the moonlight—the light associated in Dickey's work with madness and a special inner vision—the plantation owner leaves his house and his "thin wife" and "seeks the other color of his body." The speaker recognizes the very real passion in the relationship between the white man and the black woman, whether in the past or in the present:

> My body has a color not yet freed:
> In that ruined house let me throw
> Obsessive gentility off;
> Let Africa rise upon me like a man
> Whose instincts are delivered from their chains. . . .

Such passion is good, alive; yet it grows out of power over other human beings.

Furthermore, when in his ancestor's time this passion creates "A child who belongs in no world," the slave master responds with indifference. For the present-day speaker this uncaring attitude is his region's greatest sin. He cannot imagine heartlessly confining a child to a life as a doorman, waiter, parking lot attendant, or member of a road gang simply because the father will not acknowledge his son. In *Self-Interviews*, Dickey states that "the main thing I characterize as the emotion of love is the wish to protect the other person."[7]

BUCKDANCER'S CHOICE

Since the slave owner ignores the requirement to protect the black woman and their child, his guilt is profound.

In "Slave Quarters" Dickey evaluates the extremely ambivalent feelings he has about his region's history. As he states in his essay "Notes on the Decline of Outrage," every white Southerner must appraise the attitudes that he retains from his past: "Not for a moment does he entertain the notion that these prejudices are just, fitting, or reasonable. But neither can he deny that they belong to him by inheritance, as they belong to other Southerners. Yet this does not mean that they cannot be seen for what they are, that they cannot be appraised and understood."[8] However, as in "The Firebombing," the appraisal in order to be honest must convey all the ambiguities that remain.

"Them, Crying"[9] clearly embodies the wound motif that operates throughout Dickey's poetry, and, like "Slave Quarters," it emphasizes the writer's unconditional compassion for children who suffer. About this subject he feels no ambivalence. In his portrait of a truck driver who spends his nights in hospitals comforting sick and dying children, he therefore describes a man who does not scrutinize his motives—a desire for absolution or sentence—but instead simply acts.

Dickey writes, "I've always had the most complete horror of hospitals. . . . I view hospitals as charnel houses. . . . I hold it against doctors that they're not miracle workers; they're helpless in so many ways. . . . To me, the voice of a child who is alone, frightened, and in pain is an appeal so

powerful that it can go through any barrier and be heard anywhere."[10] His own feelings about children in pain become
those of his protagonist, an outsider who is "Unmarried, un-
childlike, / Half-bearded and foul-mouthed" but who at night
is "called to by something beyond / His life," the appeal of
hospitalized children. The trucker's personal characteristics
make him seem one unlikely to feel concern for others; in fact,
Dickey purposely has selected a figure who is ordinarily
thought of as insensitive and boorish. Acutely aware that he
does not belong within the medical and family groups in the
hospital, the truck driver nonetheless consoles children in
ways doctors cannot;

> For our children lie there beyond us
> In the still, foreign city of pain
>
> Singing backward into the world
> To those never seen before,
>
> Old cool-handed doctors and young ones,
> Capped girls bearing vessels of glucose,
> Ginger ward boys, pan handlers, technicians,
> Thieves, nightwalkers, truckers, and drunkards
> Who must hear, not listening, them:
> Them, crying: for they rise only unto
>
> Those few who transcend themselves,
> The superhuman tenderness of strangers.

Unlike most of those who gather in the hospital, the trucker
"transcends" himself in agonizing for a small child's return to
life. And his unselfish, unambivalent response provides the

BUCKDANCER'S CHOICE

miracle that helps the child "rise," either to health and life or to heaven as an angel.

Returning to a more ambiguous figure in "The Fiend,"[11] Dickey reasserts the tone dominating much of *Buckdancer's Choice.* Here his protagonist is both evil and good: the conventional view of the voyeur is mirrored by the poem's title; yet in its course the fiend also becomes a source for love. Fusing the potential for violent death with the possibility for transforming love, the beholder bestows a rare gift—both threatening and promising—upon those he watches:

> Not one of these beheld would ever give
> Him a second look   but he gives them all a first look that goes
> On and on   conferring immortality while it lasts

As he watches people through their apartment windows, he sees and participates in the familiar dramas of their lives:

> In some guise or other he is near them when they are weeping without sound
> When the teen-age son has quit school   when the girl has broken up
> With the basketball star   when the banker walks out on his wife.
> He sees mothers counsel desperately with pulsing girls face down
> On beds full of overstuffed beasts   sees men dress as women
> In ante-bellum costumes with bonnets   sees doctors come, looking oddly
> Like himself. . . .

He learns to read their lives as he reads their lips, "like reading the lips of the dead." And as he crouches in tree limbs, calming dogs and connecting with birds and other creatures of nature's night, he observes people who involve themselves only with the artificial, lifeless images reflected by their television screens. His is a passionate connection; theirs is passive and empty.

Yet his greatest gift and greatest threat goes to those lonely, too often unnoticed women whose husbands and lovers do not provide the intensity of emotion the fiend offers. When he watches "a sullen shopgirl" undress to shower, for example,

> She touches one button at her throat, and rigor mortis
> Slithers into his pockets, making everything there—keys, pen
> and secret love—stand up.

The thematic fusion of love and death is dramatically suggested through the rigor mortis image. However, when he "gets / A hold on himself" sexually, the shopgirl senses a connection with her unseen admirer, and she is transformed:

> With that clasp she changes   senses   something
>
> Some breath through the fragile walls   some all-seeing eye
> Of God   some touch that enfolds her body   some hand come up
>   out of roots

Once she is "beheld" she becomes "a saint" and "moves in a cloud." She sings, "As if singing to him, come up from river-fog," and is changed into an ideal of womanhood, into a goddess. For this girl as well as for all the other people he observes, "It is his beholding that saves them."

On the other hand, to those who close their shades and refuse disclosure to him, he harbors an implicit threat of danger, of possible death. Such harm will, he knows, finally emerge when he moves from his hidden existence into an open declaration of who and what he is. He will follow a closed-shade shopgirl home and into her apartment to behold her directly. And once he abandons his secret life for an open disclosure, the fusion of love and death will probably culminate in his raping and killing the one he beholds.

With the figure of the voyeur as his protagonist the poet ventures far from the conventional bounds of morality. "The Fiend," like "Slave Quarters," formulates a complex vision of human passions and their potential, a vision far removed from traditional concepts of love. And because this vision is complex, it underlines the ambiguities Dickey perceives in his world.

"The Shark's Parlor"[12] portrays one of nature's fiends, the shark—a creature who, like the snake, represents for the poet the power of indifferent, inexorable destruction. Yet like its human counterpoint in "The Fiend," the shark in this work also has transforming powers for the human being who confronts it. Dickey says the poem recounts a coming-of-age experience.[13] Clearly, however, what the protagonist learns through his struggle with the shark is that victories over the powers of death are bound to be transitory.

As the poem begins, the adult speaker invokes "Memory" to recall the time in his youth when he and his friend, Payton Ford, had fished for a shark from the porch of a beach house. Fortified by their "first brassy taste of / beer" and their nightly dreams of "the great fin circling / Under the bedroom floor,"

UNDERSTANDING JAMES DICKEY

the two spread blood upon the sea to lure the creature to their hook. The struggle between the caught shark and the boys, helped by other "men and boys," is a monumental one. Although they finally drag him onto the porch and into the house, he nearly destroys their "vacation paradise":

                              cutting all four legs from under the dinner
         table
With one deep-water move   he unwove the rugs in a moment
      throwing pints
Of blood over everything we owned   knocked the buck teeth out of
      my picture
His odd head full of crushed jelly-glass splinters and radio tubes
      thrashing
Among the pages of fan magazines   all the movie stars drenched in
      sea-blood.

And as the protagonist says:

Each time we thought he was dead   he struggled back and smashed
One more thing   in all coming back to die   three or four more
      times after death.

By triumphing over this creature of the deep, the speaker seems to have attained manhood, seems to have defeated the mindless powers of death and destruction. Yet, as he reveals at the end of the poem, he has felt compelled to buy the beach house under which the shark still symbolically swims and which he can still symbolically wreck. The narrator thus concedes that his youthful struggle with death has been—and will continue to be—forced upon him: he feels "with age / . . . in all worlds the growing / encounters." His triumph therefore

BUCKDANCER'S CHOICE

remains equivocal; the initiation experience contains real ambivalence for him.

Throughout *Buckdancer's Choice* Dickey raises difficult questions about his own and his speakers' roles in relationship to the events and people in their lives. That he comes up with no clear answers—no clear verdicts of absolution or sentence—may at first suggest that he is avoiding his responsibility as an artist. However, his stance in fact reveals his honesty, his integrity, his refusal to reduce complex issues through simple answers. By probing and finally accepting the ambiguities of his situation, Dickey opens the way to renewal, for which he continues to strive in the succeeding collections.

Notes

1. *Babel to Byzantium* 291.
2. *Buckdancer's Choice* (Middletown, CT: Wesleyan University Press, 1965) 11–20; *Poems 1957–1967* 181–88.
3. *Self-Interviews* 137.
4. *Buckdancer's Choice* 21–22; *Poems 1957–1967* 189–90.
5. *Buckdancer's Choice* 63–65; *Poems 1957–1967* 226–27.
6. *Buckdancer's Choice* 73–79; *Poems 1957–1967* 234–39.
7. *Self-Interviews* 148.
8. *Babel to Byzantium* 274–75.
9. *Buckdancer's Choice* 31–33; *Poems 1957–1967* 198–200.
10. *Self-Interviews* 141–42.
11. *Buckdancer's Choice* 68–72; *Poems 1957–1967* 230–33.
12. *Buckdancer's Choice* 39–42; *Poems 1957–1967* 205–08.
13. *Self-Interviews* 146.

CHAPTER FIVE

Falling *and* The Eye-Beaters, Blood, Victory, Madness, Buckhead and Mercy

In the preceding volumes Dickey has moved through logically evolving explorations of his themes, all of them predicated upon his conception of his own role as a survivor. *Into the Stone, Drowning with Others*, and *Helmets* chronicle various stages—recognition, identification, protection—in his movement from lacerating to self-animating guilt. Yet he begins to achieve the latter state only in *Buckdancer's Choice*, where, as in "The Firebombing," self-condemnation is replaced by uncertainty about his own judgment against himself: absolution may be as possible as sentence; an almost paralyzing sense of his own responsibility for the many deaths he has encountered may be superseded by a renewal into a new life. Both *Falling* and *The Eye-Beaters, Blood, Victory, Madness, Buckhead and Mercy* represent further steps in this process. *Falling* reveals Dickey's perhaps most sustained attempts to rise to the renewed life, while *The Eye-Beaters* plots a tendency to move inward where the new Self finally must reside.

In *Falling*, which appears as the final section of *Poems 1957–1967*, guilt begins to take on a new meaning for the poet.

FALLING AND *THE EYE-BEATERS*

Dickey asserts in "Adultery" that "Guilt is magical"; it is magical in that it becomes a source of intensifying experience and, consequently, a means of qualified affirmation. The poet begins to put away thinking in terms of damnation or relief from damnation, and instead initiates the process described by Lifton as "bringing oneself to life around one's guilt." This movement has, as he shows, tremendous implications: "Above all, animating guilt is a source of self-knowledge—confirming Martin Buber's dictum that 'man is the being who is capable of becoming guilty and is capable of illuminating his guilt.' In illuminating one's guilt, one illuminates the self. . . . It presses beyond existing arrangements, toward new images and possibilities, toward transformation."[1]

In *Falling* Dickey concentrates on instances of rising to and falling from great heights. The rising and falling motif shows the poet turning guilt into an element to aid his transformation into a new life, to add to the self-knowledge that helps him rise beyond or fall from one life into another. The first poem in the *Falling* section of *Poems 1957–1967* is "Reincarnation (II)," in which a sedentary man is reborn as a soaring sea bird; the final poem in the volume is "Falling," which dramatizes a stewardess's plunge from an airplane. Other poems repeat this rising or falling pattern. In "The Bee," a father saves his child with a diving tackle; "Bread" focuses on flyers who support themselves on the wings of their airplane after having been shot from the skies; in "Dark Ones," people go home and "fall / Down" in their "souls to pray for light / To fail"; Jane MacNaughton jumps to her death in "The Leap"; a horse and rider both fall into a creek bed in "Sustainment;" and in "Power and Light" a man ascends tall telephone poles to connect human voices by day and then descends into the darkness of his house's basement by night. Perhaps the most extensive rising and falling imagery occurs in the introductory poem of *Poems 1957–1967*—a work which, like *Falling*, had its first book appearance in the collection. In "May Day Sermon to the Women of Gilmer County, Georgia, by a Woman Preacher Leaving the Baptist Church" the speaker warns about a fall from grace, which ironically allows for a rise into a fuller life for the fallen. To accomplish such rising and falling Dickey frequently depends on the process of reincarnation, or exchange of identity, as illustrated in the first poem of *Falling*.

"Reincarnation (II)"[2] is a companion work to "Reincarnation (I)" in *Buckdancer's Choice*. Dickey declares: "Reincarnation is one religious idea I have always loved believing in. I don't know whether the soul passes from one kind of creature to another; I hope it does. I would live this human life gladly if I knew I was going to be a bird—next time—or have any kind of consciousness at all."[3] "I'd like to be some sort of bird, a migratory sea bird like a tern or a wandering albatross. But until death, until this either happens or doesn't happen, I'll have to keep trying to do it, to die and fly, by words."[4]

"Reincarnation (I)"[5] focuses on a dead Southern judge who returns to life as a diamondback rattlesnake, a transformation that comments humorously on the man's former life and the standard of Southern justice; in "Reincarnation (II)" the evolutionary process involves a man who becomes a sea

FALLING AND *THE EYE-BEATERS*

bird. While a human on earth, he has lived with "a clean desk-top" in the "hell of thumbs." His life of working in an office has been boring and routine. Yet his attraction to an existence beyond himself has not been entirely buried by his mundane life:

> I always had
> These wings   buried deep in my back:
> There is a wing-growing motion
> Half-alive in every creature.

The dormant, incomplete wings in man's back indicate his physical readiness for his spiritual liberation, his flight into nature and paradise. When he is transformed into a bird, he gains "the sense of the galaxies / . . . / Drawing slowly for him a Great / Circle." Once his transformation is complete, he becomes part of the eternal circle of life returning from death, for

> to be dead
> In one life is to enter
> Another   to break out   to rise above   the clouds

However, the man's rebirth as a sea bird does not finally move him into the paradise the poet has earlier envisioned in "The Heaven of Animals." The albatross exists in a cold void, "utterly alone," with only the prospects of a mate and of death awaiting him. The bird flies in emptiness comparable to the office prison the man experienced before becoming a bird. The man and the bird—like the mullet the albatross feeds on who believe they are free to do as they wish—move through lives prescribed by real or self-created nets. The sea bird flies through the stars that cast invisible threads around him. The final, universal net that ensnares all, however, is death:

> The dead rise, wrapped in their wings
> The last thread of white
> Is drawn from the foot of the cliffs

Death follows the sea bird, hovers near him, waiting for the opportunity to change him again.

Though it grants an opportunity for life beyond death, reincarnation in the poet's view achieves only a qualified triumph over death; one still must die to be reborn, and the transformed creature is itself subject to death. The reincarnation of man as albatross is an undeniably glorious one, a movement beyond mere human confinements. However, the heaven—the transformation—achieved also contains snares cast by death, and thus the poet discerns that reincarnation repeats rather than solves the difficulties of the previous life. As a tool of liberation, then, reincarnation is only partially successful.

Two works—the family poem "The Bee" and the war poem "Bread"—invest images of rising and falling, of transformation, with a less ambiguous meaning than does "Reincarnation (II)." In "The Bee"[6] a seemingly insignificant insect assumes the powers of the shark and snake in dramatizing how vulnerable to nature—and to death—humans can be. Yet the poem also reveals how transformation can thwart death. The quiet walk of a father and son beside a multilane highway in California suddenly turns into a race against disaster when

FALLING AND *THE EYE-BEATERS*

a bee stings the boy, causing him to run hysterically toward the oncoming traffic. As he rushes after his child, the father hears his former football coaches shouting, urging him to be "better / Than you are." The father does become better than he ever was as a halfback, for through his diving tackle he saves his child. The voices of the dead—those voices that have assumed angel-like status—help the protagonist rise, through his dive, above his middle-aged, out-of-shape body. The coaches' voices "live in the air . . . live / In the ear / Like fathers." The speaker's saving of his child grants them both a renewed life, literally for the child and metaphorically for the adult. The transformation is complete, for following the pair's withdrawal into the woods, where the boy sleeps in his father's arms, the speaker pays homage to those fatherlike figures who have helped him, saying prayerfully to one coach in particular, "Coach Norton, I am your boy." Fathers save sons, and renewal is at least momentarily achieved.

So, too, is renewal revealed through the pervasive rising and falling imagery of the war poem "Bread."[7] Its speaker is a pilot "who had not risen, but just come down / From the night sky" to share a meal with a crew of "Old boys newly risen from a B-25 sinking slowly / Into the swamps of Ceram." To keep from drowning the downed crew had buoyed themselves up on the airplane's wings, which sank slightly each time they moved to kill the snakes and lizards they ate while waiting to be rescued. Now, back in camp, the men eat the military fare: "Bread / Is good . . . I closed my eyes / I ate the food I ne'er had eat."

The last line of the poem echoes "It ate the food it ne'er had eat" from Coleridge's "The Rime of the Ancient Mariner," a line which recounts the albatross's encounter with Christian spiritual sustenance. The albatross is a soul from God that leads the sailors to safety through ice-packed seas. In Dickey's poem the saved men eat food that offers them personal and social communion with their rescuers and leads them to know the peace of survival, if only temporarily. As an image, bread is an ordinary food that rises and falls in order to reach completion. Bread is also, of course, representative of the body of Christ in the Christian communion and signals Christ's newly risen body in every man. However, this poem is not a Christian parable set in wartime but a statement about the heroic acts that took place seemingly every day among ordinary men who rose to great heights of courage. The commonplace food they eat takes on special significance when related to their extraordinary deeds that become commonplace. In one respect this poem serves almost as the poet's personal reassurance that those who were in the war deserve much more than an unresolved question about their absolution or sentence, the quandary so wrenchingly dramatized in "The Firebombing." The speaker and the men share their bread gratefully, glad to be alive; but the bread that truly sustains them is their shared companionship and their survival, at least for a little while.

Renewal is not so easily won in two major love poems— "Adultery" and "The Sheep Child"—of *Falling*; however, in these treatments of forbidden love Dickey again overturns common assumptions about the nature of guilt. In "Adultery"[8] both

FALLING AND *THE EYE-BEATERS*

the pain and the fulfillment of the lovers result from their flout-
ing of conventional morality. "We have all been in rooms / We
cannot die in, and they are odd places, and sad," the poem begins. With this line are introduced fear of death and pervasive
sadness, moods reinforced by repeated references to the couple's weeping, to the uncertainty of their vows—"I will see you
next week / When I'm in town. I will call you / If I can"—and
to the necessary sterility of their sexual connection:

> Nothing can come
> Of this   nothing can come
> Of us.
>
> . . . .
> Nothing will come of us.

The lovers meet in motel rooms decorated by vulgarly
romantic pictures: Indians offer themselves at sunrise to the
Great Spirit, cattle graze and look on with "the eyes of our
children," men drive the last golden railroad spike. The pictures seem to mock the romantic expectations of the lovers,
yet in the face of banality, sterility, and sadness, the two do
achieve a moment of passion:

> But we would not give
> It up, for death is beaten.
> . . . .
> One could never die here
>
> Never die   never die
> . . . .

> We have done it again   we are
> Still living.   Sit up and smile,
> God bless you.   Guilt is magical.

Guilt is magical, as Dickey explains, because it provides a "heightening of sexuality" that in turn produces a "temporary alleviation of the terrible death fear that grows on people as they get older and older."[9] Thus, in this poem guilt ultimately—if only momentarily—effects a kind of renewal, the transformation of the lovers from sterile, pain-stricken, fallen adulterers to living, smiling, risen beings.

"The Sheep Child"[10] is certainly the most startling of Dickey's love poems, dealing as it does with possible consequences of human-animal sexual contact—"this monstrous, clandestine marriage," as the poet labels it.[11] The poem relates the story that somewhere in an Atlanta museum

> There's this thing that's only half
> Sheep   like a woolly baby
> Pickled in alcohol. . . .

The terrifying legend is designed to keep

> Farm boys wild to couple
> With anything   with soft-wooded trees
> With mounds of earth   mounds
> Of pinestraw

from copulating with animals. Such myths help the boys to adopt more conventional moral patterns: *They groan   they wait   they suffer / Themselves, they marry, they raise their kind.* The sheep child, imprisoned in its jar of

FALLING AND *THE EYE-BEATERS*

alcohol and *"In the minds of farm boys,"* is a horrifying emblem of human guilt and fear.

Yet the second half of the poem, narrated by the sheep child, recounts the special, if guilt-fraught, love that existed between the boy and the ewe, who gave *"her best / Self to that great need."* Their offspring, Dickey declares, is "evidence of the blind and renewing need for contact between any kind of living creature with another kind."[12] And the sheep child is endowed with a vision *"Far more than human"*:

> *I saw for a blazing moment*
> *The great grassy world from both sides,*
> *Man and beast in the round of their need,*
> *And the hill wind stirred in my wool,*
> *My hoof and my hand clasped each other,*
> *I ate my one meal*
> *Of milk, and died*
> *Staring.*

Guilt drives the farm boy to more conventional sexual behavior, but it also—and perhaps more importantly—forces him to confront the nature of his "great need" and responsibility. In this sense guilt offers at least partial renewal in the form of increased self-understanding.

"Power and Light,"[13] one of the most significant of the social poems in *Falling*, recounts the literal and symbolic rise and fall of its narrator. In his daily work as a lineman he ascends poles to connect people, to aid long-distance human connection. As a private man, however, he climbs down from the poles and, when arriving at home, climbs down into his

UNDERSTANDING JAMES DICKEY

dark basement to his own source of power—whiskey—and drinks heavily, yelling for his wife to "CLOSE THE DOOR between / The children and me." In his private life he communicates with his family from an even greater distance than that confronting the people whom he connects through wires.

His existence at home is a figurative burial in the underworld of his basement, his drunkenness, and "Years in the family dark." Yet although he is self-exiled and numbed by drink, while beneath the earth he can feel "all connections," just as the protagonist in "Drinking from a Helmet" knows that the dead, underground, wait for "all their hands / To be connected like grass-roots." In his private underworld he perceives that "pure fires of the Self / Rise crooning in the lively blackness."

After he awakens in the morning and passes through the kitchen, that "sad way-station," he again climbs poles, laughing, while his "charged hair" stands on end, connecting human voices that pierce "To the heart." Beneath him he sees that "Far under the grass of my grave, I drink like a man / The night before / Resurrection Day." Ironically, his own resurrection occurs when he descends into darkness, which again ironically is his personal source of "power and light," the source of his knowledge that "the dark is drunk   and I am a man / Who turns on. I am a man."

Laurence Lieberman correctly identifies this figure as "an emblem for the artist."[14] Carl Jung perhaps best described the artistic personality's conflicts caught in Dickey's dramatization of the lineman: "Every creative person is a duality or a

FALLING AND *THE EYE-BEATERS*

synthesis of contradictory aptitudes. On the one side he is a human being with a personal life, while on the other side he is an impersonal, creative process. . . . The artist's life cannot be otherwise than full of conflicts, for two forces are at war within him—on the one hand the common human longing for happiness, satisfaction and security in life, and on the other a ruthless passion for creation which may go so far as to override every personal desire."[15] As the protagonist in "Power and Light" asserts, "Never think I don't know my profession / Will lift me." His true source of power and light, however, occurs in the private underworld of his own hell, his own symbolic nightly death and rebirth. In his bravado he suggests a possible—if not entirely attractive or successful—mode of renewal.

Like "Power and Light" the nature poem "For the Last Wolverine"[16] focuses on both destructive and creative forces in man. Such figures as road builders, railroad crews, and fur trappers mindlessly have driven the wilderness to the brink of extinction. Yet the speaker wills nature—in a supernatural form—to fight back. The sub-Arctic setting of the poem provides a pervasive whiteness that suggests Melville's mysterious veil separating man from nature. Into this setting the speaker would have the last wolverine eat his "last red meal of the condemned," thereby nourishing himself with an idea of how to survive. The protagonist would have him climb the last spruce tree and mate with "The New World's last eagle," and from such a mating would come an offspring similar to mankind's Christ, a magnificent beast that would become na-

UNDERSTANDING JAMES DICKEY

ture's savior. Enormous and ferocious, the creature would scream that it "cannot die" and would ride "into holy war against" destructive mankind.

Significantly, the narrator appeals to the "Dear God of the wildness of poetry" to let such a beast be born. The wolverine's and all of nature's struggle for survival against hostile forces is linked directly to the poet's requirements for poetry:

> How much the timid poem needs
>
> The mindless explosion of your rage,
>
> The glutton's internal fire   the elk's
> Heart in the belly, sprouting wings,
>
> The pact of the "blind swallowing
> Thing," with himself, to eat
> The world, and not to be driven off it
> Until it is gone, even if it takes
>
> Forever.

Nature's struggle against extinction is comparable to the poet's battle against the artistically artificial, the "suspect in poetry." Each struggle is difficult but elevating.

"For the Last Wolverine" fuses the three main thematic elements in Dickey's relationship with nature: the protagonist feels a spiritual affinity with the wild creatures' battle for survival; he learns a further dimension of poetry's artistic requirements; and, finally, he gains a vision of nature's potentially final moments. The wolverine does not mate with the

FALLING AND *THE EYE-BEATERS*

eagle to create a marvelous bestial savior; instead, the earthly creature remains "small, filthy, unwinged, / . . . crouching / Alone," a "bloodthirsty / Non-survivor." Yet, says the poet, "I take you as you are / And make of you what I will," an emblem of the poet's and the wolverine's pervasive desire for survival, for renewal. The poem's last line thus functions as a prayer for both the animal and the artist:

> *Lord, let me die   but not die*
Out.

The title poem of *Falling*, which is also the final poem of the 1957-1967 collection, seems closely connected in theme and technique to "May Day Sermon," the introductory work of *Poems 1957–1967*. Each has as its protagonist a woman who rises or falls from her previous existence, and her experience is expressed through religious and sexual imagery. Each, too, is extremely long-lined, as if the actions and emotions expressed explode conventionally restrictive poetic forms. The lines break, rhythmically and graphically, so that key words and ideas are juxtaposed to create meanings—and variant meanings—in single phrases:

>   she screaming   her father screaming
Scripture   CHAPter and verse   beating it into her with a weeping
Willow branch. . . .

These lines from "May Day Sermon" illustrate the technique: The irate father is not merely screaming at his daughter as he beats her but is "screaming / Scripture"; he is not performing his violent act "with a weeping" but "with a weeping / Willow branch." These juxtapositions enhance the ambiguities of the poem. Moreover, both "May Day Sermon" and "Falling," like many of Dickey's poems, rely heavily on verbal constructions—especially gerunds and present participles—that give immediacy to the experiences being set forth. And each poem, like the others in *Falling*, reveals protagonists trying to attain a renewed life.

Based on a *New York Times* story of a 29-year-old stewardess who was swept through the emergency door of an airborne plane, "Falling"[17] turns the facts of a senseless, macabre accident into an astonishing testimony to human efforts for survival. Thrust from her safe, ordered world of "the galley with its racks / Of trays" into the chaos of the world outside, the stewardess goes through successive stages of helpless terror, of determined strategies to save herself, of resigned preparation for her fate. She will, of course, die as she slams into the prairie earth, but through her performance and the images it evokes in the minds of those sleeping in the farmhouses below, she becomes—as a symbol of human mortality and human aspiration—"the greatest thing that ever came to Kansas."

Plunging through the blackness of the void toward the lights of farms and autos, the woman in her best moments attempts to gain control of her descent and of herself: *"One cannot* just *fall   just tumble screaming all that time   one must* use / *It."* She adopts characteristics of flying creatures—hawks, owls, bats, even a human skydiver who she momentarily imagines might save her. She envisions diving into water, the "saving / Element"; but as this possibility disappears, she first loses, then regains, control:

```
                                   she comes back from flying to falling
Returns to a powerful cry
. . . . . . . . . . . . . . . . . . . . . . . . . . . . . . . . . . . . .
                             nearly      nearly losing hold
Of what she has done      remembers      remembers the shape at the heart
Of cloud      fashionably swirling      remembers she still has time to die
Beyond explanation.
```

Her death ritual, like that of Donald Armstrong in "The Performance," becomes a "last superhuman act"; but in "Falling" it is expressed through both sexual and religious imagery. As her final preparation for death the woman strips away her clothes, including the "sad impotent wings" of her stewardess's jacket, and prepares to "come openly" among the widowed Kansas farmers and young boys and girls whose dreams she has entered as "goddess" and "holy ghost / Of a virgin." Literally her body will lie deep "in the earth as it is in cloud" (an ironic echo of a line from the Lord's Prayer) and the hoped-for "waters / Of life" will become "the far waters / Of life," eluding and ultimately failing her. Yet in the imaginations she has entered, she survives as a sexual and religious symbol of renewal. Moreover, as the last lines of the poem reveal, her great effort to live continues to the end:

```
Feels herself go      go toward      go outward      breathes at last fully
   Not      and tries      less      once      tries      tries      AH, GOD—
```

So, too, in "May Day Sermon to the Women of Gilmer County, Georgia, by a Woman Preacher Leaving the Baptist Church"[18] is a fall viewed as a means of salvation for a woman—and, in this case, for womankind. As in "Falling" a protagonist is swept by forces beyond her control from an apparently ordered world into a chaotic, potentially death-dealing, but infinitely richer one. Here, however, the secure place is not an airplane with its racks of trays but instead the Baptist Church with its laws and restrictions; the force is not sheer accident but instead irresistible natural urgings; the new world is not the void and the Kansas soil but instead the fog-encircled wilds of passionate sensuality.

The text of the woman preacher's sermon focuses on a dramatic fall from grace. An enraged, Bible-quoting farmer, discovering that his daughter has made love to a one-eyed, motorcycle-riding mechanic, drags her to the barn, ties her to the centerpole, and brutally beats her with a willow branch while screaming scripture. Following the beating the naked girl staggers to the farmhouse, where later that night she plunges an ax into her father's head and an ice pick through one of his eyes. She then runs to the barn and frees all the animals before leaping onto the back of her lover's motorcycle and disappearing with him into the night and the fog.

The girl has clearly fallen from the grace of the Baptist Church through her sexual transgression and the murder of her father; yet through the oratory of the woman preacher—who, as the title declares, is herself in the process of leaving the church—the girl's acts take on a wholly different meaning. The

FALLING AND *THE EYE-BEATERS*

minister evokes traditional Christian imagery: the father, in her account, screams "like God / And King James as he flails," and the girl is "WHIPPED for Bathsheba and David   WHIPPED for the / woman taken / Anywhere   anytime." The father thus assumes the force of a patriarch of the church, and the daughter is associated with wayward, punishable figures. However, the preacher also structures her sermon around a repeated phrase, "Each year at this time," and although the repetition is consistent with fundamentalist oratory, its message is not. Each year at this time, the minister declares, woman is seized by natural sensuality which forces her to break the restrictive laws of her church. As Thomas Sloan indicates in his essay on this poem, the preacher therefore exhorts her sisters in the congregation "to rise up and meet not the Eternal Bridegroom but the very real and earthly lover, to answer the call of the spirit that moves through all nature and renews itself each spring."[19] Thus, the young girl's—and the woman minister's—fall from grace in the fundamentalist Christian sense signals their ascension into a grace of a more natural kind.

Throughout *Falling* Dickey employs images of rising and falling, of reincarnation and transformation, to suggest his— and his protagonists'—continued movement toward renewal. In this volume guilt is not entirely lacerating, self-condemning, but is instead at least partially animating, "magical." The poems in *Falling*, however, like many of the earlier poems, tend to focus on figures who are not entirely identifiable with the poet himself. *The Eye-Beaters, Blood, Victory, Madness, Buckhead and Mercy*, on the other hand, sets forth a central

UNDERSTANDING JAMES DICKEY

speaker who seems very similar to Dickey in character and concerns. This volume dramatizes the poet's movement inward, a movement that explores his own Self in an attempt to bring himself as near renewal as possible. Yet such a renewal proves more difficult to achieve than that won by the rescued airmen, transformed stewardess, or saved woman preacher.

The literary Self appearing in *The Eye-Beaters* is protean—evolving, changing from poem to poem—yet throughout the volume the speaker looks back at his life to determine what it has been and has become. In many of the poems of this book the protagonist is aging and physically ill, a fact that forces him to internalize the possibility of death rather than examine it in relation to others. Furthermore, several of the poems examine relationships—with family, with friends, with lovers—that are painfully subject to the destructive powers of time. The speaker's increased consciousness of his own inability to defeat time and death produces the unusually solemn tone of *The Eye-Beaters*.

In three works of the volume—"Knock," "Diabetes," and "The Cancer Match"—the protagonist is assaulted by forces that are both outside and within him. "Knock"[20] features a sudden pounding on the door "in the quick dead middle / Of the night," a sound which produces in the speaker terror and confusion:

> is the code still
>
> The same can the five fingers
> Of the hand still show against
> Anything?

FALLING AND *THE EYE-BEATERS*

In the two poems that compose "Diabetes"[21]—"Sugar" and "Under Buzzards"—the protagonist adopts more positive, if varying, stances in regard to the force that threatens him. "Sugar" reveals him combatting his illness by following his doctor's orders to exercise:

> Each time the barbell
> Rose   each time a foot fell
> Jogging, it counted itself
> One death   two death   three death and resurrection
> For a little while.

"Under Buzzards" shows him considering whether to abandon all treatment, to allow his blood "To stream with the death-wish of birds." In "The Cancer Match"[22] the speaker concedes that

> I don't have all the time
> In the world, but I have all night.
> . . . .
> And I have cancer and whiskey.

On this night at least the whiskey—the fuel of "my joy, my laughter, my Basic Life / Force!"—will defeat the illness. Yet here, as in the other poems of fear, aging, and disease, the protagonist clearly recognizes that he has achieved resurrection only "For a little while."

The perception that life is infused with death is perhaps most dramatically set forth in "Victory,"[23] the volume's single war poem. Set in Okinawa and Yokohama just after V-J Day, "Victory" reveals a narrator who is celebrating two birthdays,

his literal one and his symbolic one: "I was ready to sail / The
island toward life / After death." He has survived the war—"it
was foretold / That I would live"—and he is affirming his existence with a bottle of whiskey, a gift from his mother.

Yet as he drinks he recalls an earlier birthday in the jun-
gles of New Guinea where, drunk on another gift of whiskey,
he had hallucinated a snake's head emerging from the bottle.
The creature, communicating to him "The Allied victory to
come," had thus become an emblem of "the angel / Of peace."
Now, naked and alone among his former enemies in a Yokohama tattoo parlor, the narrator acquires an enormous snake-
skin tattoo. It begins at his throat, cuts through the sunburned
V on his chest, and coils around his stomach, hips, and thighs.
As the design nears completion, man and snake become one
being; they share the protagonist's head, and "our hearts /
Beat as one."

By adopting this new skin the speaker is signaling his
rebirth, his "escaping / Forever   surviving   crushing
going home"; he has fulfilled the earlier snake's prophecy of
victory and survival. Yet because in Dickey's world the snake
is always equated with death, the narrator's grafting of the
creature's skin upon his own suggests that in the new life he
will continue to be haunted by death. Ironically, then, "the angel of peace," "the new prince of peace"—man and snake com-
bined—carries the imprint of both survival and destruction.
And, as the speaker repeats three times in his victory poem, "I
can't help it."

FALLING AND *THE EYE-BEATERS*

This rather dark perspective also clearly influences the tone of two family poems—"Butterflies" and "Giving a Son to the Sea"—joined under the title "Messages."[24] The works show the protagonist at play with his sons, but in each case the games involve very real risks. In "Butterflies," for example, the father and his oldest son "play, and play inside our play" on top of an earthen dam. Their actions are characterized by "pure abandon," a phrase repeated four times in the poem. Yet against this kind of play is set another—gambling—which carries significant risks. Discovering the skeleton of a cow that contains thin bones "like shaved playing cards," the narrator sits in the "hearse" of the skeleton and then returns to his son who has fallen asleep while watching butterflies:

> That is all, but like all joy
> On earth and water,
> in bones and in wings and in light.
> It is a gamble.

Within their joy lies the possibility of its failure, its symbolic death. Similarly, in "Giving a Son to the Sea" the speaker realizes that the relationship he has shared with his younger son must also change. At the age of six the boy had fired at his father's heart a toy bullet bearing the message "I love you." Now the growing child has a passion for the sea—"the real / Wonder and weightless horror / Of water"—and the father realizes that he must relinquish his hold on his son: "I must let you go, out of your gentle / Childhood into your own man suspended / In its body." In such a realization lies very real pain and fear.

The narrator hopes that the boy will magically discover a new world under the sea,

> will find us there
> An agonizing new life, much like the life
> Of the drowned, where we will farm eat sleep and bear children
> Who dream of birds.

Whatever the case, however, the speaker remains resigned to but saddened by the inevitable changes in his relationships with his son.

"Two Poems of Going Home"[25]—"Living There" and "Looking for the Buckhead Boys"—also treat a middle-aged narrator's sense of change and loss. In "Living There" the protagonist calls himself "The Keeper," an accurate description since he maintains two households: the childhood home that now "lives only / In my head" and the adult home that he presently shares with his wife and sons. Yet as he considers that both his first house and his own father—"Blue-eyed   blue-eyed   the fixer   the wagon-master"—are now in actuality gone, he is overwhelmed by the transience of the world and of human life. Realizing his own present house and family will also soon be gone, he cries out in pain at his own powerlessness:

> Why does the Keeper go blind
> With sunset? The mad, weeping Keeper who can't keep
> A God-damned thing   who knows he can't keep everything
> Or anything alive: none of his rooms, his people
> His past, his youth, himself,
> But cannot let them die? Yes, I keep

FALLING AND *THE EYE-BEATERS*

Some of those people,
. . . .
I think I know—
I know them well. I call them, for a little while, sons.

Although he finally suggests that his present home and he himself may be "kept" in the memories of his sons, he qualifies any true optimism by the phrase "for a little while."

The same theme dominates "Looking for the Buckhead Boys," in which the narrator returns to his hometown in hope of resurrecting his past, his youth. Yet even with his first line—"Some of the time, going home, I go / Blind and can't find it"—he admits the difficulty of his quest. Most of the town's old landmarks have changed or disappeared, and, as the speaker learns from the hardware merchant while consulting "the Book of the Dead"—"the 1939 / North Fulton High School Annual," the majority of the Buckhead Boys have met with only trivial success, if not absolute disaster. His one hope lies in finding Charlie Gates, who once had been half-blinded by lime in his eye during a football game and who now operates a local gas station. Meeting Charlie, who squints at him through the fumes of his Gulf gasoline, the speaker silently cries, "Charlie, Charlie, we have won away from / We have won at home / In the last minute." Yet the message is sent in "code," and the narrator cannot be sure that his old friend truly sees or understands his plea when he says, "Fill 'er up. Fill 'er up, Charlie.'" The suggestion is that the past cannot be resurrected, that the speaker cannot stop time from eroding and clearing away "for further development" what once was home. Thus his sense of loss is intensified.

The love poem "Mercy"[26] treats yet another antidote for pain, another possible source of renewal for the narrator; but the imagery of the work suggests that, once again, this effort to connect is not entirely successful. In Mercy Manor, the nurses' dormitory that is both "whorehouse / And convent," the protagonist meets his lover, Fay, who as a nurse seems to offer medical and sexual healing. Dressed in white she combats "the long cry" of suffering and death, the mortality that "wails out" over Saint Joseph's Hospital; dressed in black she prepares to induce the "wail like all / Saint Joseph's" that accompanies the speaker's lovemaking. Strong and capable—"a hard / Working worker for Life"—Fay tries to save him just as she tries to save those who suffer in the hospital. And to some extent she succeeds:

> we sink
> Down flickering
> . . . .
> happy
> About everything   O bring up
> My lips   hold them down don't let them cry
> With the cry   close   closer   eyeball to eyeball
> In my arms, O queen of death
> Alive, and with me at the end.

However, the merging of happiness and crying, of life and death, suggests that the narrator's release through love is neither complete nor permanent.

FALLING AND *THE EYE-BEATERS*

"The Eye-Beaters"²⁷ continues the hospital setting of "Mercy" but casts the speaker as an artist. While observing blind children who have had their arms bound to their sides to prevent them from beating flashes of light into their unseeing eyes, the protagonist engages in an internal debate involving his reason and his imagination. Reason insists that the children see nothing, that *"There is nothing inside their dark,"* *"nothing but blackness forever."* Imagination asserts that "the blind must see / By magic or nothing" "the original / Images of mankind." As the children are unbound and returned to their wards, the speaker hears their eye-beating yells, not for mercy but rather for "pure killing fury   pure triumph pure acceptance." He therefore forces himself to embrace the position of his imagination, grasping that both the blind children and the artist must finally adopt "the sheer / Despair of invention." Both must create light out of their own darkness, when in reality there may be nothing to see.

The stance of the artist is also clearly reflected in both of the nature poems—"Apollo" and "Pine"—appearing in *The Eye-Beaters*. "For the First Manned Moon Orbit," the initial section of "Apollo,"²⁸ celebrates the fusion of imagination and technology:

> You and your computers have brought out
> The silence of mountains the animal
> Eye has not seen since the earth split, . . .

"The Moon Ground," the second section of "Apollo," focuses on a single astronaut-speaker who, as he picks up moon rocks, feels as if he and his companions are "The only men" in the universe. Significantly, the protagonist's sense of isolation conjures up questions about earth: "What hope is there at home / In the azure of breath, or here with the stone / Dead secret?" He can provide no answer but instead recalls "Gray's Elegy," a poem emphasizing man's aloneness and anonymity. Finally, however, like the artist of "The Eye-Beaters," he simply asserts himself—"eyes blind / With unreachable tears"— and picks up moon rocks to be carried back to earth.

"Pine"[29] employs what Dickey labels "associational imagery,"[30] which here seems designed to increase the reader's sensual perceptions of the object. Subtitled "successive apprehensions," the poem traces the speaker's attempts to understand the tangible and intangible features of the tree. The work's five parts illustrate the stages of the protagonist's progression toward "glory." In Parts I and II he experiences a primitive, sensual response to the wind in the tree, the "breath" of the tree that suggests freedom. The wind creates a series of aural images that in turn cause the tree and the man to assume amorphous shapes: "Low-cloudly it whistles, changing heads / On you. How hard to hold and shape head-round." When the narrator inhales the air that has blown through the tree, he changes into a pinelike figure, "Tarred as a stump and blowing / Your skull like clover." He further unites himself with the tree in Part III: "another life of you rises, / A saliva-gland burns like a tree." He eats a wafer of bark and wonders whether the part of the tree he absorbs will be passed on to his future children. Ignoring the bitterness of the pine's taste and enduring various sorts of pain as he climbs into the rough-barked tree to its top, the speaker, in Parts IV and V, embraces "It all":

> A final form
> And color at last comes out
> Of you alone putting it all
> Together like nothing
> Here like almighty

V

> Glory.

Here the combination of art and nature does seem—at least temporarily—to bring the narrator wholeness.

"Turning Away,"[31] the final poem in *The Eye-Beaters*, is a fitting conclusion to the volume. Subtitled "Variations on Estrangement," the poem focuses on a narrator who realizes that "Something for a long time has gone wrong, / Got in between this you and that one other." At first glance it appears that "you" and "that one other" are, respectively, the speaker and his weeping wife; however, the fracture in the marriage simply reflects a fracture in the narrator's own being. Gazing through a window he contemplates his reflection superimposed upon a meadow scene outside. His image suggests "a king starting out on a journey / Away from all things that he knows." The narrator wishes to "Prepare to fight / The past," to "Change; form again; flee."

Yet as he watches his potentially heroic reflection, it slowly alters. Chickweed outside appears to drape his image in choking hair, causing "Iron-masked silence" and a "deadly, dramatic compression" within his mind and heart. He stands isolated, bound by his personal history, and unable to make new and meaningful connections, as his successive imaginings show. Throughout the poem he envisions himself as a soldier, but all he can hope for in this guise is "a helmet of silent war / Against the universe." He imagines himself as lover to women of all races and times who thereby will found a vast new generation of beings, but he is called back from his reverie by the weeping of his wife, and "Despair and exultation / Lie down together." He dreams that nature may provide him with healing answers, but all it yields is "its secret / Of impassivity, unquestionable / Silence." His potential sources of renewal failing him, the narrator at the end of his poem stands "on guard" rehearsing what he "will answer / If questioned" about his life. Yet he strongly suspects that such knowledge can come only "Later, much later on."

In *Falling* Dickey creates figures who begin the process of renewal. Significantly, however, these figures—stewardess, sheep child, lineman—are clearly not Dickey himself. When, as in *The Eye-Beaters*, the poet creates middle-aged, ailing, time-haunted protagonists who more closely resemble himself, he finds renewal more difficult to achieve. Appropriately, his desire to "Change; form again; flee" is accomplished when he adopts a form new to him, the novel. And the deliverance

FALLING AND *THE EYE-BEATERS*

thereby won becomes a permanent feature of the later volumes of poetry.

Notes

1. Lifton, *Home from the War* 128.

2. *Poems 1957–1967* 243–51.

3. *Self-Interviews* 140.

4. *Self-Interviews* 79.

5. *Buckdancer's Choice* 29–30; *Poems 1957–1967* 196–97.

6. *Poems 1957–1967* 279–80.

7. *Poems 1957–1967* 265–66.

8. *Poems 1957–1967* 259–60.

9. "Comments to Accompany *Poems 1957–1967*," *Barat Review* 3 (January 1968) 9–15.

10. *Poems 1957–1967* 252–53.

11. *Self-Interviews* 165.

12. *Self-Interviews* 165.

13. *Poems 1957–1967* 256–57.

14. Laurence Lieberman, "The Worldly Mystic," *Hudson Review* 20 (Autumn 1967) 513–20.

15. Carl Jung, "Psychology and Literature," trans. W. S. Dell and Cary F. Baynes, *The Creative Process*, ed. Brewster Ghiselin (Berkeley: University of California Press, 1952) 225.

16. *Poems 1957–1967* 276–79.

17. *Poems 1957–1967* 293–99.

18. *Poems 1957–1967* 3–13.

19. Thomas O. Sloan, "The Open Poem Is a Now Poem: Dickey's May Day Sermon," *Literature as Revolt and Revolt as Literature* (Minneapolis: University of Minnesota Press, 1969) 93.

20. *The Eye-Beaters, Blood, Victory, Madness, Buckhead and Mercy* 37.

UNDERSTANDING JAMES DICKEY

21. *The Eye-Beaters* 7–9.
22. *The Eye-Beaters* 31–32.
23. *The Eye-Beaters* 38–41.
24. *The Eye-Beaters* 10–13.
25. *The Eye-Beaters* 17–23.
26. *The Eye-Beaters* 14–16.
27. *The Eye-Beaters* 50–55.
28. *The Eye-Beaters* 25–30.
29. *The Eye-Beaters* 44–46.
30. *Sorties* 96.
31. *The Eye-Beaters* 56–63.

CHAPTER SIX

Deliverance

H ow Dickey changes and forms again is dramatically demonstrated in his only novel to date, *Deliverance*. In this work his protagonist achieves the renewal—the deliverance— for which the writer has struggled throughout his poetry. The speaker is able to find a new order, a new connection, a new sense of real well-being that becomes his passionate affirmation of life. Because the economy of language required in poetry does not allow for the expansive analysis that fiction provides, it is understandable that Dickey most fully develops this transforming function of survivor's guilt in his novel.

The ordeal shared by the four suburbanites who travel down the river in *Deliverance* clearly parallels that confronting the soldier in combat. In the first chapter of the novel, "Before," the suburbanites are revealed as quite ordinary men leading quite ordinary, inconsequential lives; they, like raw recruits, have not tested their courage or themselves. During the central three chapters—"September 14th," "September 15th," and "September 16th"—they are brutalized both by the wild river and by vicious mountain men; in order to survive they, like soldiers, must conquer and kill their enemies and must witness death in their own ranks. Finally, throughout the last chapter, "After," survivors of the trip must come to terms with their death encounters; they must, like combat veterans, weigh their responsibilities for the deaths they have caused and observed. Such is the process that protagonist Ed Gentry goes through as he seeks and ultimately attains deliverance.

The "Before" section of the novel establishes the individual characters and histories of the four suburbanites. Bobby Trippe, who works with mutual funds, is the figure most acclimated to city life. Popular and social, he is "a pleasant surface human being," though Ed has once seen him blow up at a party with "the rage of a weak king"[1]. Bobby is the least inclined of the four to take the canoe trip through the wilds. Drew Ballinger, who seems to regard nature as a picturesque location for mountain musicians, is a solid citizen and company man: "He worked as a sales supervisor for a big softdrink company and he believed in it and the things it said it stood for with his very soul" (9). Drew also becomes a spokesman for the laws of civilization during the trip. That he has a son bearing "some kind of risen hornlike blood blister on his forehead that his eyebrow grew out of and around in a way to make you realize the true horrors of biology" (9) should warn him about nature's defiance of man's laws; yet Ballinger remains a naïve though well-intentioned man.

Lewis Medlock, who lives on the revenues of inherited rental properties, devotes himself wholeheartedly to fitness in order to be prepared for the time when "the whole thing is go-

DELIVERANCE

ing to be reduced to the human body, once and for all" (42). He wishes to test himself to see if he is capable of withstanding or triumphing over the wilderness in its most primitive state: "You might say I've got the survival craze, the real bug" (43). What he prepares for is his own immortality, his victory over man and nature and death. He approaches the experience of the weekend trip armed with primitive weapons—a bow and arrow, a knife, and a canoe. But his most important weapon, he feels, is his "values" (48), his mental attitude, which earlier had enabled him to crawl unassisted out of the woods with a painfully broken ankle. Lewis admires the "dependability" (47) of the mountain people in equipping themselves for the rigors of a natural, primitive existence, even though they are "ignorant and full of superstition and bloodshed and murder and liquor and hookworm and ghosts and early deaths" (49). Lewis becomes Ed Gentry's primary instructor in the art of surviving nature's—and man's—violence.

Ed, the narrator-protagonist, is a "get-through-the-day-man" who is "mainly interested in sliding" (41). He has reduced his work, his relationships, and, indeed, his entire life to the "mechanical": "I was a mechanic of the graphic arts, and when I could get the problem to appear mechanical to me, and not the result of inspiration, I could do something with it. . . . And that, as far as art was concerned, was it" (26–27). He is pleased with the idea of the unpressured, "no-sweat shop" (13) that he and his partner run, yet the description suggests a place of little real commitment. And, in fact, he scorns would-be artists who, "like George Holley, my old Braque man," say,

"I am with you but not of you" (15). Even with his wife, Martha, who believes more in his talent than he himself does, Ed responds primarily to her "normalcy"—her "toughness that got things done," her "practical approach to sex" (28)—rather than to the "absolutely personal connection" (26) that she has once offered. Like many of the figures in Dickey's war poetry Ed is imprisoned, but his primary cage is his sense of his life's worthlessness: "The feeling of the inconsequence of whatever I would do, of anything I would pick up or think about or turn to see was at that moment being set in the very bone marrow. . . . It was the old mortal, helpless, time-terrified human feeling" (18).

The nature of the wilderness that these four suburbanites enter is suggested by the mountain people they encounter in the town of Oree. Physically and mentally twisted by intermarriage, inadequate health care, and the hardships of their lives, these inhabitants of "the country of nine-fingered people" (56) seem hostile toward the city dwellers. Drew shares a guitar-banjo duet with an albino boy who has "pink eyes like a white rabbit's; one of them stared off at a furious and complicated angle. That was the eye he looked at us with, with his face set in another direction. The sane, rational eye was fixed on something that wasn't there, somewhere in the dust of the road" (58–59). Although Ballinger and the boy make musical connection, no other sort is invited. Furthermore, as the suburbanites negotiate with—and antagonize—the Griner brothers, who reluctantly agree to deliver Lewis's car to Aintry, Ed notes the Hadeslike environment of the mountain men's garage:

It was dark and iron-smelling, hot with the closed-in heat that brings the sweat out as though it had been waiting all over your body for the right signal. Anvils stood around or lay on their sides, and chains hung down, covered with coarse, deep grease. The air was full of hooks; there were sharp points everywhere—tools and nails and ripped-open rusty tin cans. . . . and through everything, out of the high roof, mostly, came this clanging hammering, meant to deafen and even blind (62).

The imagery of the description explicitly conveys the danger these men and others like them pose to intruders from another culture.

The river itself, the Cahulawassee, offers both threat and promise to the suburbanites. Like the rivers and streams of Dickey's poetry it functions as a pathway to death as well as to life. Entering the Cahulawassee, the four men note its pollution—a severed chicken's head reminds Ed of a human head—and throughout their trip the men are battered by its force. Yet when Gentry first steps into the water to free his canoe from rocks, he senses its positive power: "It felt profound, its motion built into it by the composition of the earth for hundreds of miles upstream and down, and by thousands of years. The standing there was so good, so fresh and various and continuous, so vital and uncaring around my genitals, that I hated to leave it" (75). Embracing his sexual-creative parts, the river provides his baptism into nature. This experience is confirmed by an encounter Ed has that night when an owl lands on his tent roof. He touches its talon, and he then imagines that he hunts with the bird as it repeatedly leaves and returns to his tent: "I hunted with him as well as I could, there in my weightlessness. The woods burned in my head. Toward morning I could reach up and touch the claw without turning on the light" (89).

The connections between man and river, man and bird, signal the beginning of Gentry's movement from the civilized world into the world of nature. As he awakens next morning and prepares to hunt while the others sleep, he realizes that in this place "none—or almost none—of my daily ways of living my life would work" (93). He begins to abandon his habit of sliding; and walking through a dense river fog "exactly to my teeth" (96), he seems to disappear and then reemerge into a new state of being. However, he badly misses his bow-and-arrow shot at a deer, revealing that he is still a novice, still only partially formed.

Later the same morning comes the encounter with nature—and with nature's men—that puts Ed and his friends to their first real test. Gentry and Bobby, who share a canoe, become separated from the other pair because of Bobby's ineptness. Growing tired of fighting the waters, of "learning the hard way" (107), they decide to rest in the apparent safety of the riverbank. They find there, instead, the real threat of two mountain men whose appearance and movements suggest

DELIVERANCE

Dickey's earlier descriptions of snakes and sharks, his embodiments of absolute but indifferent evil:

One of them, the taller one, narrowed in the eyes and face. They came forward, moving in a kind of half circle as though they were stepping around something. The shorter one was older, with big white eyes and a half-white stubble that grew in whorls on his cheeks. His face seemed to spin in many directions. . . . The other was lean and tall, and peered as though out of a cave or some dim simple place far back in his yellow-tinged eyeballs (108).

Nature's men in nature's setting sodomize Bobby and threaten Ed. But when one of the men tells Ed to "Fall down on your knees and pray, boy. And you better pray good" (116), Gentry's prayer is answered not by God but instead by Lewis, another of nature's creatures, who shoots the older man through the chest with his bow and arrow and frightens the other man into the woods. Clearly in this setting life is reduced to its simplest terms; in the wilderness, as in combat, man kills or is killed.

What action should follow, however, is not so easily resolved by the suburbanites, and each man's position indicates the degree to which he is bound by civilization's conventional beliefs. Drew, for example, says that they should "Listen to reason" (130), that they have committed "justified homicide" (121), and that the legal system will give them a fair trial if they tell "the whole story" (121). Lewis, at the other extreme, dismisses Drew's views as "boy scoutish" (123); he declares that the men themselves are the law, that "no body, no crime" (125), and that there is "not any right thing" (123) except what they determine is right. When asked for his opinion, Bobby fulfills Ed's earlier description of his having "the rage of a weak king" by repeatedly kicking the mountain man's corpse in the face.

While the others argue, Gentry tries to define his own position by turning to the river: "I tried to think ahead, and I couldn't see anything but desperate trouble, and for the rest of my life. . . . I could feel myself beginning to breathe fast in the stillness. . . . I listened to the woods and the river to see if I could get an answer" (123–24). Like the combat veteran, Ed realizes that this death encounter will stay with him forever, and his appeal to nature further confirms the transformation occurring within him. Finally the four agree to bury the dead man, conceal their actions, and live with the guilt they share. In killing the man they have done what they had to do, they decide, and only Drew believes that confession would save them. Yet like the combat-veteran speaker in "The Firebombing," they are uncertain about whether ultimately they should be granted absolution or sentence for their actions.

After the men have buried the mountain man and started down the river again, Ed concedes that "something came to an edge in me. . . . A gigantic steadiness took me over . . . that added up to a kind of equilibrium" (139). This equilibrium is tested by disastrous events. The men are thrown into the river, and Ed feels the life-threatening nature of his second baptism: "I turned over and over. I rolled, I tried to crawl along the flying bottom. Nothing worked. I was dead. I felt myself fading out into the unbelievable violence and brutality of the river, joining it. . . . I got on my back and poured with the river, sliding over the stones like a creature I had always contained but never released" (144). This experience marks his full recognition of nature's power and of men's proper relationship with it: not to fight it but to merge with it, adopt its methods. Ed's realization comes at exactly the right moment, for Drew has been killed—possibly by a shot from the cliffs above the river—and Lewis, the group's leader, has broken his leg. Ed therefore must assume command, and he feels infused with a new inner power: "I liked hearing the sound of my voice in the mountain speech. . . . It sounded like somebody who knew where he was and knew what he was doing" (152–53).

That Gentry has achieved oneness with nature is revealed through his climb up a mountainside to hunt the surviving mountain man, who may or may not be stalking the suburbanites. Before he begins his ascent, Ed again approaches the river:

Then for some reason I stepped into the edge of the river. In a way, I guess, I wanted to get a renewed feel of all the elements present. . . . I stood with the cold water flowing around my calves and my head back, watching the cliff slant up into the darkness. More stars had come out around the top of the gorge, a kind of river of them (156).

His vision fuses river, mountain, and stars, and as he begins his ascent, he himself connects with the natural elements. In the darkness he finds himself in a dreamlike state, one in which he becomes a wary but sensitive lover of the mountainside: "With each shift to a newer and higher position I felt more and more tenderness toward the wall. . . . I turned back into the cliff and leaned my mouth against it, feeling all the way out through my nerves and muscles exactly how I had possession of the wall . . . in a way that held the whole thing together" (163). Ed's connection with the cliff is throughout expressed in sexual terms. Furthermore, several times during his ascent he has dangerous slips; "Often a hand or foot would slide and then catch on something I knew, without knowing, would be there, and I would go on up" (177). Because his instincts are now thoroughly those of nature, he can find the secure spots without actually seeing them. He had earlier evidenced some of this same ability by making contact with the owl and its talons, but here his sense is much more fully developed.

As he attains the summit, Gentry casts himself and the mountain man in nature's predator-prey relationship: "I'll make a circle inland, very quiet, and look for him like I'm some kind of animal. What kind? It doesn't matter, as long as I'm quiet and deadly. I could be a snake" (174). He thinks as the mountain man thinks—"our minds fuse" (180)—and adopts the cold "indifference" of both the man and nature. He predicts where his prey will emerge from the woods, climbs carrying bow and arrow into a tree, and, using his graphic designer's sense in a new way, creates a pattern which only the mountain man can complete. That the stranger does, in fact, enter that precise spot may at first seem an unconvincing manipulation of plot; yet Dickey clearly intends it to show how completely Ed has

DELIVERANCE

become nature's predator who is able to read the mind, foresee the actions, of his prey. And as the stranger steps into Ed's mechanical design, the picture becomes in a very real sense a work of art, allowing Ed to say, "I had never seen a more beautiful or convincing element of a design. I wanted to kill him just like that" (189). Gentry's shot is true, but with it he falls out of the tree and wounds himself in the side with his remaining arrow, and he has to track down the man, who has stumbled into the woods. Finding his prey dead, Ed declares, "His brain and mine unlocked and fell apart" (199); the protagonist is no longer exclusively a predator.

Whether he has killed the right man remains unclear. Ed cannot positively identify the man as his would-be sodomizer and murderer; nor can he be certain, later in the novel, that the man is the deputy sheriff's missing brother-in-law. Neither can he or the other survivors be sure, when they find Drew's body, that he has been killed by a rifle shot. Because they cannot know the truth, they decide to bury both bodies in the river and thereby avoid legal inquiries. The question of right and wrong remains, but Dickey purposely leaves it unanswered. *Deliverance* is not a simple morality tale of violation and revenge; it is a story of men who must learn to live with uncertainty about their own guilt or innocence. They, like the speaker in "The Firebombing," cannot know whether they deserve absolution or sentence.

Yet in the novel, for the first time in his work, Dickey creates a figure who does achieve complete renewal. Ed Gentry outwits the authorities who await the men at the end of their canoe trip, and following a final drink of water from the river he returns to the family and the life that he feels are going to save him. However, the real salvation lies in his experiences on the river and his later appraisal of them. Ed has undergone the classic stages of survivor's guilt. He has confronted his enemy in a death encounter. He feels that he is alive because someone else has died in his place: "I had a friend there who in a way had died for me, and my enemy was there" (275). He has undergone a series of baptisms in the river and a series of exchanges helping him to merge with nature; such fusions have helped him to reorder his perspective on who and what he is. He has emerged from the fog into a renewal as a changed human being. Now he goes home to be healed and saved. Martha does help heal him physically, yet his real salvation lies within his own mind: "And so it ended, except in my mind, which changed the events more deeply into what they were, into what they meant to me alone" (274).

His deliverance alters Ed in his everyday life. He abandons his role as a "slider" and becomes instead a man with purpose. He now takes himself seriously as an artist, identifying with the office's one other serious artist: George Holley "has become my best friend, next to Lewis, and we do a lot of serious talking about art" (276). His office now displays the work of Braque as well as "headlines of war and student strikes" (276). And although Bobby returns unchanged to the "affable, faintly nasty manner he always had" (276), Lewis also learns an important lesson about himself. He discovers that "he can die now; he knows that dying is better than immortality. He is

DELIVERANCE

a human being, and a good one" (277). Lewis and Ed have learned how to gain real control over their lives; each now is able to become "the author of [his] own life story,"[2] as Lifton phrases it.

Lewis describes his archery as "passing over into Zen. . . . You shouldn't fight it. Better to cooperate with it. Then it'll take you there; take the arrow there" (278). His description applies also, of course, to the lives of these two men. Rather than wrestling with questions of their personal innocence or guilt, they submit to the flow of their lives as if carried by the river that now runs only in Ed's mind:

The river and everything I remembered about it became a possession to me, a personal, private possession, as nothing else in my life ever had. Now it ran nowhere but in my head, but there it ran as though immortally. I could feel it—I can feel it. . . . In me it still is, and will be until I die, green, rocky, deep, fast, slow, and beautiful beyond reality (275).

The river becomes a private, haunting emblem of experiences that have transformed Ed Gentry, have delivered him into a new life.

Notes

1. *Deliverance* (Boston: Houghton Mifflin, 1970) 9. The page references within the text are to this edition.

2. Lifton, *Home from the War* 393.

CHAPTER SEVEN

The Zodiac,
The Strength of Fields,
and Puella

T|o keep his vision exciting to himself and to his readers
Dickey has, throughout his career, pursued new forms, new
voices. In the poetry following *Deliverance* this tendency toward experimentation becomes increasingly apparent. The
novel seems to have granted its author a vehicle for exploring
fully the process of confrontation, reordering, and renewal in
his characters and himself. Having worked through this process, he then is able in *The Zodiac, The Strength of Fields,* and
Puella to achieve his goal stated in "Turning Away"—to
"Change; form again."

The Zodiac, Dickey's first major publication following
Deliverance, is a long poem treating the role of the artistic
imagination in comprehending the universe. With its first line
the work announces its concern with renewal: "The man I'm
telling you about brought himself back alive / A couple of
years ago".[1] Although this man, Hendrik Marsman, may not
prove successful in sustaining his life, the work reveals a Dickey who is experimenting with new voices, new techniques.

THE ZODIAC through *PUELLA*

The poem is, as Dickey explains in his headnote, based on another work of the same title by a Dutch poet, Marsman, who died in a North Atlantic torpedo attack in 1940. In Dickey's version Marsman becomes the protagonist. Drunk and hysterical, he seems to reflect both the political chaos of Europe in the later 1930s and early 1940s and the personal chaos of the man who would be poet-seer. The choice of a European speaker is new to Dickey's work, but even more importantly this voice is fused with that of a second speaker—an omniscient "I"—who sometimes interprets, sometimes seems to share, Marsman's experiences. This technique, too, is somewhat unusual in Dickey, although finally unsuccessful: at many points in the poem the reader cannot tell which narrator is speaking and thus cannot stringently plot the development of either. *The Zodiac* is clearly an ambitious work, an effort to achieve new perspectives, but ultimately it proves less artistically satisfying than either the earlier or later poetry.

The poem is divided into 12 parts, suggesting thereby a correspondence with the 12 signs of the zodiac. However, no such pattern actually exists. Instead, the work is structured around the perceptions and experiences of the protagonist. Part 1, which comprises almost half the work, establishes Marsman's character and situation—his grappling with questions of time, history, and the universe; his frustration, anger, drunkenness, and despair. Parts 2 through 7 chronicle the Dutchman's more specific probings of the limitations of the human intellect. Such intellectual systems as mathematics and philosophy cannot, he decides, penetrate the secrets of the universe. In Parts 8 through 11 Marsman—employing dreams, memory, and fantasy—examines his own personal history; here he abandons strict reason for the more expansive imagination. Part 12 finds Marsman at peace with his universe and himself. He now determines that he will "steer this strange craft" (61), his life and art.

The Zodiac clearly dramatizes Dickey's belief that the artist's expansive imagination is the truest means of grasping the secrets of the universe. Although Marsman gives God, the master artist, poor reviews for his drawing of the figures in the constellations—"A child could do better," he says (44)—the Dutchman does admire the austere beauty and mystery of their design. He recognizes that the God who created such configurations is a vital source for mortal, temporal artists such as himself. Marsman wishes to connect his own sexual, creative parts, his "balls" (29), with those of the divine being so that he can perceive and perhaps re-create that "some sort of meaning" (12) in the constellations. He asserts that it takes a poet, a special visionary man, to accomplish this goal.

Yet, struggle as he may, he cannot quite penetrate the abstruseness of God, of nature:

> The
> *secret—*
> Is whiteness.   You can do *anything* with that.   But no—
>   The secret is that on whiteness you can release
>   The blackness,
>   The night sky.   Whiteness is death   is dying
> For human words to raise it from purity   from the grave
>   Of too much light. (21)

THE ZODIAC through *PUELLA*

Whiteness here, as in "For the Last Wolverine," suggests nature's mask to keep man from discovering its secrets; whiteness also describes the blank page that stares back at the poet. Both nature's and the page's blankness terrorize Marsman and drive him to seek relief and inspiration in drink, *acquavit*—potato alcohol, and perhaps the water of life. In his drunken state Marsman finds neither answers nor the poetic muse but instead hallucinates a gigantic lobster designed to challenge God's zodiac. However, the lobster, turning on its creator, threatens to claw him to bits. Finding no answers to the divine and mortal questions that plague him, the protagonist ends the long first section with a key question: "Words. / How?" (30). How, he wonders, can he overcome the blankness of the page? How can he create words that truly express all that he knows and all that he agonizes to know?

His life on earth, in contrast to that represented by God's expansive zodiac, is contained within the walls of his small, single room: "a priest's failed prison-cell" (10). His only decoration is a triangular mobile representing "human shattering-art" (18), a man-made imitation of the three-point connection the philosopher Pythagoras perceived among the sun, moon, and stars. Pythagoras has taught Marsman to see through "triangular" eyes with which "the stars are beaten down by drunks / Into the page" (25). The poet's admiring but angry relationship with God is duplicated by his dual attitude toward Pythagoras: at times Marsman rages at him by saying, "You've driven me nuts enough with your music of the spheres!" (22); at other times he acknowledges the philosopher's perception of the universe as an eternal wheel. However, most of all Pythagoras represents what Marsman opposes.

Pythagoras believed that the key to the cosmos was contained in what Marsman calls "insane mathematics" (44). The philosopher contended that the harmony of the universe, the music of the spheres, was based on an elaborate mathematical formula that quantified virtually everything in the universe. In Pythagorean terms numbers are a way of explaining man's existence, his history, his concept of time. Such a view of man in relationship with the eternal or divine is the primary prison cell that Marsman feels he must escape and transcend.

As a poet Marsman looks outside his room and sees real creatures, potential subjects: "Look right out over town. / Real birds. There they are in their curves" (20). He wonders if he has been trying to write about the wrong subjects, has read the wrong books, has thought the wrong thoughts in his quest for artistic expression and understanding. Yet "he can't get rid of himself enough / To write poetry" (20); that is, he cannot shake the limitations imposed on himself and the world by the insane mathematics of those like Pythagoras. Such scientists-philosophers, Marsman feels, have imprisoned God and time and reality in the cells and triangles of reason. "God / Whirls slowly in man's numbers   in the gilded Gothic / Of thorn-spiked Time" (32–33), while time itself is "just an uncreated vertigo / Busted up by events" (33). Marsman's explanation of how man has mistakenly mechanized and misunderstood time also suggests how man has restricted his understanding of experience, of history, of thought, and, consequently, of the universe:

> What do *wheels* and *machinery* have to do with Time?
> With stars?
> . . . .
>   Overhead in the midst of Nothing,
> Is the very clock for a drunk man. For the Lord also? (31)

God's eternal zodiac, rather than man's clocks and numbers, is the true means of governing experience, for without the zodiac time would not exist—that is, true, "present time" (42).

Marsman's shift in focus, in Part 8, from the universal expanse of God's heavens to his own personal history illustrates how the visionary poet records experience and gains meaning from such events. His life has been a series of wanderings through dreams and memory as well as through actual events. He looks into the darkness of his own life, thereby creating nightmares; these nightmares, in turn, evolve into images of fire, the element that Pythagoras believed was at the heart of the cosmos and that is, in Marsman's view, at the heart of his vision. Out of these nightmares, memories, and drunken hallucinations Marsman dramatizes his past.

Returning in actuality and memory to the home of his youth, he sees the room where "his mother twisted pain to death / In her left breast" (51). He also locates the spot where as a child he had hidden in leaves because of a young girl's rejection of his love, a rejection which had, in turn, caused him to fill "His diary with dreadful verses" (52). The rocks in this landscape advise him never to come back: "Don't wander around your own youth. / Time is too painful here. Nothing stays with you / But what you remember" (54), while "forgetting. . . . It's that thing you might call death" (38). Here Marsman reaffirms that one's personal history depends upon memory, that the absence of memory is equivalent to death. Futhermore, he suggests, the passage of time is designated not by numbers but by human feelings—love, pain, or whatever one truly experiences during his life.

By extension, what is true for Marsman and his method of comprehending his own history is applicable to all men. In the final scene of the poem his tone changes from near hysteria to a quiet affirmation and acceptance. He has tried to, but cannot, discern the mysteries God has hidden from man. He turns away from such pursuits and concentrates on different matters to explore in his life and art. He asks his soul to "put me in a solar boat. / . . . / Bringing quietness and the rare belief / That I can steer this strange craft" (61). The craft that Marsman refers to could be either the ship on which he will meet his death, torpedoed in the North Atlantic, or the craft which conveys his art of writing. These possibilities exist as part of his determination that he will through his poetry

> Make what it can of what is:

> So long as the spirit hurls on space
> The star-beasts of intellect and madness (62).

Marsman moves toward the eternal, the divine, in his "craft" while relying on intellect and madness—the twin ingredients of the visionary poet as he moves toward light and "the morn-ing / Land that sleeps" (61).

Dickey has frequently voiced his belief that as an artist he should strive for new methods of expressing his vision. Such a demand has helped him achieve magnificent successes; at the same time, it has caused him to risk real failure. *The Zodiac* fi-nally does not succeed as well as the poet or his readers would hope. Yet in the work Dickey has broken the confines of a for-mer Self, a former method, and has moved toward renewal in his vision and his art. Such a renewal greatly benefits the vol-umes that follow. Marsman's concluding tone—an accepting affirmation—carries over into *The Strength of Fields*. The im-agery conveying Marsman's "intellect and madness" clearly influences the haunting lyricism of *Puella*.

The quietly contemplative and accepting voice in *The Strength of Fields* illustrates the extent to which the healing process has helped the poet gain an acceptance of himself and of his new life. As Richard J. Calhoun and Robert Hill declare, kindness defines the theme and tone of the collection,[2] an idea demonstrated by a passage from the title poem:

> More kindness will do nothing less
> Than save every sleeping one
> And night-walking one
>
> Of us.

Divided into two parts, the volume in its first section pro-vides poems offering further development of subjects explored in Dickey's first six volumes. The second section, which makes up about one-third of the collection, contains his translations, the merging of his own poetic voice with those of other writers. Filtered through Dickey's personality and methodology, these works seem cooperative ventures rather than translations. Laurence Lieberman states in his review: "His first translations . . . break new ground in the art of translating the poetry of foreign tongues ("unEnglish") into his native tongue. . . . We sense a wizardry of infinitesimal shifts and adjustments not unlike the atomic transmutations of one metal slowly alchemizing into another. Whatever the line and stanzaic pattern of the original poem, Dickey employs a characteristic spacing device to suggest the . . . magical interlocking of two voices, two languages."[3]

Although his translations are noteworthy, the works in the first section are more significant. The family poem "The Voyage of the Needle"[4] dramatizes how near the dead are to the living, how they are drawn together by small though important details. The adult protagonist duplicates a trick taught to him in his childhood by his mother: after a tissue supporting a needle becomes saturated by water and dissolves, the needle floats on the water's surface as if buoyed up by magic. Now as the speaker repeats this "magic" in his bathtub, the needle points toward his heart and becomes his heart's needle. As a device for mending, for joining two parts into a single whole, the needle connects the dead to the living: "It is her brimming otherworld / That rides on the needle's frail lake, on death's precarious membrane." The relationship of child and mother that earlier has contained a mixture of love and guilt now is transformed into a mended wholeness, a healed wound conveying "joy and glory."

Like "The Voyage of the Needle" the war poems of *The Strength of Fields* reflect Dickey's new tone of acceptance. "Haunting the Maneuvers," the first of "Two Poems of the Military,"[5] is set in a pre–World War II training camp where recruits are being "bombed" by sacks of flour dropped from planes. The speaker is "the first man killed," but because his is a sham death and "easy," his response—and the tone of the poem—is at first comic. Yet while others sleep, the "self-rising" protagonist ascends into his dream of death while hearing the laughter at the "chaplain's one / Dirty joke." The dirty joke connects to the inevitability of death in all its seriousness. Adopting the condition of the dead, the narrator says he

> can say
> Nothing but what the first-killed
> Working hard all day for his vision
> Of war says best: the age-old Why.

The answer to his questions comes in the second of the "Two Poems of the Military"—"Drums Where I Live." Here the protagonist and his family live across a lake from a military training camp which constantly seems to be "Expanding / The Range" of its drums and grenades. These civilians live their lives to the military cadence, but their war is the struggle to survive as a unit, to stay together:

UNDERSTANDING JAMES DICKEY

> Where I live, and my heart, my blood and my family will assemble
> Four barely-livable counts. Dismissed
> Personnel. . . .
> This time, this
> Is my war and where in God's
> Name did it start? In peace, two, three, four:
> In peace peace peace peace
>
> One two
>
> In sleep.

While the family count off their battles against time, the speaker tries to hold on to his son, who moves toward his own new life. Yet although the protagonist realizes that his effort will not be successful, he is finally able to achieve sleep, knowing that these wars of the heart are his reward—painful but fulfilling—for having survived actual war.

"Two Poems of Flight-Sleep"[6] reinforce the idea that Dickey's speakers achieve a kind of peace in *The Strength of Fields*. As in the other pair of war poems in the volume, the first work establishes a problem and the second provides a resolution to it. "Camden Town" features a speaker who in 1943 dreams of "letting go" and flying his training plane toward the "West," an image of peaceful death. Instead, he ultimately decides to return to the "warbound highways" of the "East," the actual war with its threat of horrifying death. In the second poem, "Reunioning Dialogue," presumably the same speaker 29 years later exchanges war stories with his former flying companion. They recall a particularly terrifying evening when they had lost contact with the convoy they flew cover for and feared being intercepted by the enemy:

> but I thought of the five boys
> From our squadron   all volleyball players
> With no heads, and all but one
> Island south of us was Japanese.

That the details of that night are so vividly remembered shows that the experience has stayed forever with them; yet the two men are now able to put it in perspective, even to treat it with comic bravado. The death imprint remains, but the protagonist and his friend are now reconciled to it.

Dickey's most eloquent statement about renewed life beyond the painful memories of war occurs in "The Rain Guitar."[7] While touring England in 1962, the speaker visits Winchester. Since he cannot locate the Cathedral, he sits beside a river in a natural cathedral, watching the eelgrass flow beneath the water's surface as it tries "to go downstream with all the right motions / But one." Like others in Dickey's poetry, this stream provides a means of connecting the living with the world of death; in this case the living include the speaker, who strums his guitar during a gentle rain, and a peg-legged fisherman, who encourages and later dances to the music. The protagonist begins to play energetically, offering Georgia mountain music, buckdancer songs, and finally an "Australian / Version of British marching songs" from World War II. The war songs bond the two men, for at the height of the speaker's playing the fisherman shouts that he was "Air Force," wounded in Burma. Their similarities—their involve-

ment in the war as Air Force men and their love of music—
promote a reunioning dialogue between war's survivors. Their
music and dance become a dramatic expression of their great
joy of having lived through combat "and improved": improved and healed their lives. In this poem the sense of renewal is explicit and exuberant.

The tone of the volume's most important nature poem,
"Remnant Water,"[8] is quite somber. The work focuses on a
man who appears to be an American Indian, a carp that un-
successfully attempts to avoid death, and a "hundred acres of
canceled water." As the speaker fishes "in my tribal sweat," he
realizes a series of losses while watching his caught fish struggle for survival in the "slain lake": "my people gone my fish
rolling / Beneath me and I die." The dead water, the dying
fish, and the diminishing Indian people are witness to the
"sound surrounding NO." All three figures have no hope for
survival, yet just as the fish struggles against the certainty of
the primal NO, so too does the man "Laugh primally" at his
and his people's disappearance. Fighting for the last vestiges of
life, they are while "dying, / Living up to it." The speaker thus
remains determined to face his downfall with strength and
without loss of dignity.

The volume's title poem, in contrast, features a man
whose life seems filled with promise. Written for and delivered at President Jimmy Carter's inauguration celebration,
"The Strength of Fields"[9] portrays the speaker alone with his
thoughts on the eve of his assuming office. As he walks over
the Southern farmland in the middle of the night, he asks him-

self and the "Dear Lord of all the fields" how to "penetrate and find the source / Of the power" which can sustain him as he takes on the heavy duties of the presidency. He appeals to the night and its stars and to the dead lying "under / The pastures"—the elements of nature and of his own history that are his heritage. And the answer comes in its "simplest" form: "More kindness." The speaker's experience parallels that defined by the poem's epigraph from Van Gennep's *Rites de Passage*: ". . . a separation from the world, / a penetration to some source of power / and a life-enhancing return."

Significantly, this movement applies not only to the poem's speaker and to the people he will serve but also to the writer himself. He has through the course of his work explored his persistent themes as a survivor, penetrated them through his evolving Self, and achieved a renewed, "life-enhancing" being. Like Ed Gentry and most of the speakers in the poems of *The Strength of Fields*, then, he has learned to cooperate with rather than fight his oppressive, haunting memories.

Puella, Dickey's last collection of poetry to date, the title of which is Latin for *girl*, is his most radical experiment with a new voice. In this volume he adopts a female perspective *"male-imagined,"* as he declares in the dedication, instead of his usual male voice; he uses a lyrical rather than narrative mode; and he prefers internal, indirect musing to external, direct drama. Tracing the development of Deborah from girlhood to womanhood, he creates a "fusion of inner and outer states, of dream, fantasy, and illusion where everything partakes of the protagonist's mental processes and creates a single impression,"[10] his definition of his general poetic method. In *Puella* the method yields a pattern of imagery related to the four elements—fire, air, water, and earth—and to sound. Yet because the speaker's musings are interior, the imagery conveying them functions much like that of the Japanese haiku: the reader himself is forced to participate in making the connection between image and emotion. That the connection is not explicitly drawn but only suggested by the writer makes *Puella* a very difficult volume.

Two poems illustrate Deborah's persistent association with the transforming element of fire. In "Deborah Burning a Doll Made of House Wood,"[11] the collection's first work, a ritualistic destruction-baptism by fire signals the speaker's coming of age. When, at her doll's funeral pyre, Deborah announces, "I am leaving," she launches her own journey into womanhood. This rite of passage carries with it the pain of loss as she watches her toy, which "As a child I believed I had grown," point "with unspeakable aliveness" toward her. Nonetheless, Deborah rises from the ashes of her childhood illusions to approach her maturity. This journey leads, in "Doorstep, Lightning, Waif-Dreaming,"[12] to her own "ground." As she sits on the doorsteps of strangers and asks if she is their child, she receives, instead of acceptance, a vision of an inner fire "full of lingering off-prints / Of lightning" that course through her mind and body. This internal fire causes her clothes to "flicker" and her "light-sensitive hairs" to tingle. She is clearly

not a child of ordinary people but instead a creature born
from inner lighting, her own "root-system of fire."

Deborah's connection with the earth is emphasized in
"Ray-Flowers (I)"[13] and "Ray-flowers (II)."[14] In the first poem
she claims "ground" as her own by appearing as a *Winged
Seed, / Descending with Others*." She spirals gently to earth
until she finds a fertile hold. In the second poem Deborah and
her sister—a figure who appears at various moments throughout the collection—are transformed from seeds into "equal-
ling / Spirits of land." They bloom into early womanhood as
flowers in a "caused meadow" extending "All the way to the
hills, / The near hills, thinning with overreach." The hills, like
male lovers, connect with the flowers in a reaching gesture
that forms a natural bond between flower and landscape.

The earth is not only the site of the speaker's sensual ripe-
ness but also, in "Deborah as Scion,"[15] the location for her
family dead, her roots. In Part 1, "With Rose, at Cemetery,"
she is revealed as an offspring—a graft of the parent—who
has grown into her own being though she acknowledges her
connection to those who lie buried in the earth:

> The dead work into a rose
> By back-breaking leisure, head-up
> Grave-dirt exploding like powder
> Into sunlit lace, and I lie and look back through their labor
> . . . .
> All over me from the green mines
> And black-holes of the family plot.

She grows on her forehead the black brows of her uncle, and she wears the family lace—"In the dead's between stitches breathing"—to which she gives the life of her own character, as have previous generations of women in her family.

In Part 2, "In Lace and Whalebone," the image of Deborah in her grandmother's antique lace further develops her relationship with a long line of women: "As I stand here going back / And back, from mother to mother: I am totally them in the / eyebrows, / Breasts, breath and butt." Her grandmother's lace is encircled with whalebone stays that hold her with their rings, becoming as well an image of the circle connecting the dead and the living: Deborah is "risen in lace" and the "ring on ring—a refining of open-work skin."

As she stands before a mirror, she envisions the violent plundering of a whale "ripped-up and boiled-down" so that she and her ancestors could wear and give individual life to this lace with its skeletal ribbing:

> I stand and think
>
>   . . . its whole lifetime on one air:
>   In lightning-strikes I watch it leap
> And welter   blue wide-eyes   lung-blood up-misting under
>   Stamped splits of astounding concentration,
>   But soundless,
> . . . .
>   And we can hold, woman on woman,
>   This dusk if no other
>   and we will now, all of us combining,
>   Open one hand.

THE ZODIAC through *PUELLA*

> *Blood into light*
> Is possible: lamp, lace and tackle   paired bones of the deep
>   Rapture

Through the destruction of this creature, as through the destruction of the doll in the initial poem, "Woman on woman" has emerged. Within this dress as well the generations of women join hands, leading her into "the one depth / Without levels, deepening for us."

In "The Lode,"[16] subtitled "Deborah's Rain-Longing," water suggests her growing sexuality. As she looks "outward" into the rain, she feels a desire for "delight / In this studied water": "Teach me / And learn me, wanderer: . . . Be somewhere within the outside   within / My naked breath. . . . / Rainfall, give me my chance." The chance this water gives her is to fulfill her sensual stirring, her natural creative and procreative dimensions as a woman.

"Deborah in Mountain Sound: Bell, Glacier, Rose"[17] dramatizes the fruition of such longings. This poem illustrates Dickey's technique of having the poem's characters incorporate objects of the setting into their own inner natures. It also demonstrates his method of lyrical indirectness. Dickey does not present the bell's ringing directly, for example; rather, the sound evokes images of a physical outline of sound. The bell's voice becomes an "Averaging-sound," a note that is "space-thinning   space-harvesting metal—/ . . . Life-longing intervals . . . / Reasonless as cloud." These qualities in the glacial mountain air mark as well the "intervals" of the lovers' "winter-lust." The three-part connection among bell, glacier, and rose, in fact, evolves into physical features of the lovers. The man feels the response desire brings within his loins as he is "inch-dreaming under the oval / Of the bell interruptedly cloven" on him. The "bell" now suggests the female sexual parts that hold his maleness, "the mason's rose / Of ice-sculpture in her fist, / Her image flash-frozen" with the "making-fluid of men." The frozen, ramming power of the glacier, the delicacy of the rose, and the bell of her sexual being combine to express intimacy between lovers.

Yet Deborah's creative expressions take more forms than merely sexual ones. "From Time,"[18] subtitled "Deborah for Years at the Piano," illustrates her ability to express her unique voice through music. Her special sound occurs from "hands that were not born completely / Matched," a fact which in turn gives her playing a "fresh, gangling resonance / Truing handsomely." As she sits at the piano, she realizes that her body is an instrument capable of resurrecting the art of such long dead creators as Schumann and Bach. Through the printed text and her own body's physical performance, Deborah's music forms a bond with the dead who are "at their workbench altars / Half-approving / time-releasing."

The volume's thematic conclusion occurs in the penultimate poem, "The Surround,"[19] a work subtitled "Imagining Herself as the Environment, / She Speaks to James Wright at Sundown." Deborah's speech to the lyric poet, who died on 25 March 1980, in fact becomes a prayer to him as he moves from life to death. At the same time Dickey draws together the important images used throughout *Puella:* the reflected echo of veer-sounds, the many circles and rings that suggest the cycle of life and death, and the fusion of fire, air, earth, and water that the young woman represents.

At dusk Deborah stands deep in the forest while the setting "sun burns / Down in pine-cone smouldering." In her mind she hears the waning sound of the last ax that disturbs the quiet, but it is a sound that now "Fails, and yet will be almost everywhere / Till midnight." The ax serves as a key metaphor in the poem, for it is comparable to Death's scythe and is seen in progressive stages—"now still half-way"—during its arc through the air. Deborah wills the dead poet to pray with his heart, the longing muscle whose music is duplicated by the bird that "in its hunting sorrows / Bides in good falling—gone / The gather-voices, and more the alone ones." She desires that in the earth around the "beginning sleeper" the footprints of predators not leave their "blood and waste" but rather their "intensified beauty / And alertness."

As day becomes night, the sunlight becomes moonlight, and the living and the dead move toward a new form of existence. After midnight, when these transformations occur, Deborah prays that now the world will have "No ax encircling you, no claw, no life-giving death / Of anything." Instead, she wishes the moon to shine "breaking and coming together, / . . . On water." As the dead man moves toward transformation, she wishes him to "Rest in soft flame," the "gentle / . . . fire" that has a "still-growing source." She requests that he stay with her—"hearing / Your hearing come back in a circle"—for now that the night has started into a new day and he has started his journey into death, "no ax / Shall be harmful to your wholeness":

> You are in your rings, and growing
> In darkness.   I quell and thicken
>   Away.   I am
>
> The surround, and you are your own.

The dead poet evolves into his own private "surround," while Deborah becomes the embodiment of "the Environment," a figure of life's wholeness.

Once Deborah becomes "the Environment," "the surround," the final poem, "Summons,"[20] brings the volume full circle to the beginning poem. In "Summons" Deborah completes the journey she undertook when she told her doll being consumed by fire, "I am leaving." Dickey includes, in one-or two-line references, the key aspects of the young woman's character presented throughout the other poems. "Summons" provides a variety of settings, beginning with a deathly swamp and ending with Deborah's carrying in her womb a real child, a replacement for the doll that grew, in her imagination, into something real. And in "Summons" Deborah answers a call from another voice, the poet's, thus, in the words of the refrain, merging in a way that allows them both to *"Have someone be nearing."* They form a union that is complete when she is "With half of my first child / With invention unending." *Puella* begins as a dramatization of a girl and concludes as the celebration of a woman, a figure that expands into the character of natural creativity that is whole and *"unending."*

THE ZODIAC through *PUELLA*

In *Puella*, then, as in *The Zodiac* and *The Strength of Fields*, new voices and new tones emerge. These collections, in one sense, complete Dickey's movement from confrontation through reordering to renewal. Yet in their originality, their sheer daring, they also suggest that for this poet—the consummate artist, the consummate risk-taker—the journey is not yet finished.

Notes

1. *The Zodiac* (Garden City: Doubleday, 1976) 9. The page references within the text are to this edition.

2. Richard J. Calhoun and Robert W. Hill, *James Dickey* (Boston: Twayne, 1983) 103.

3. Laurence Lieberman, "Exchanges: Inventions in Two Voices," *Sewanee Review* 88 (Summer 1980) 1xv-1xvi.

4. *The Strength of Fields* (Garden City: Doubleday, 1979) 23-24.

5. *The Strength of Fields* 18-22.

6. *The Strength of Fields* 30-38.

7. *The Strength of Fields* 25-27.

8. *The Strength of Fields* 28-29.

9. *The Strength of Fields* 15-17.

10. *Babel to Byzantium* 287.

11. *Puella* (Garden City: Doubleday, 1982) 13-14.

12. *Puella* 38.

13. *Puella* 27-29.

14. *Puella* 30.

15. *Puella* 31-34.

16. *Puella* 41-42.

17. *Puella* 37.

18. *Puella* 39-40.

19. *Puella* 45-46.

20. *Puella* 47-48.

CHAPTER EIGHT

Dickey as Critic

S oon after Dickey's early reviews and essays were collected and published as *The Suspect in Poetry* Richard Kostelanetz labeled him "unquestionably the finest critic of American poetry today. . . . Dickey is gifted with the knack of turning a review into a significant essay, in which real ideas are stated, large-scale judgments are made, overall interests defined, analyzed, evaluated and questioned."[1] Yet as Richard J. Calhoun notes, Dickey often has been perceived as a kind of "hatchet man," a Southerner railing against the invariably Northern, typically traditional "establishment."[2] Calhoun in fact refutes this notion in his essay, one of the best assessments to date of the poet as critic. Nonetheless, his statement and Kostelanetz's illustrate the extreme responses raised by Dickey's criticism.

These contradictory responses—positive and negative—no doubt result from Dickey's uncompromising honesty in setting forth standards for both his own and others' poetry. They are standards that have remained consistent throughout the years. He is suspicious of apparent artificiality, either in

DICKEY AS CRITIC

subject matter or technique, and he condemns the poetic stance that seems to belittle or ignore the audience. He becomes impatient with those who write highly skilled, polished verse yet do not risk new methods, do not develop. As Calhoun says, the central theme of *Babel to Byzantium* is "the relationship between the poem and the inner life of the poet. Dickey believes each poet has his own vision, his Byzantium."[3] And if he does not remain true to that vision, or if he presents a less-than-genuine performance in any way, Dickey contends, the poet fails himself, his art, and his audience.

The relationship among writer, poem, and reader is indeed of central importance to this poet-critic. Such an equation may at first seem overly obvious; yet for Dickey a poet's failure to fulfill his commitment to his craft and to his audience usually is the result of a lack of honesty concerning his literary Self, or of an imprecision in language, or of an inability to move the reader deeply. These failures create in turn what Dickey terms the "suspect": "Almost all poetry contains elements that are suspect, having no relation to what the readers believe in as 'reality,' and even in a sense of degrading it by offering experience as a series of unbelievable contrivances, none of which has the power of bringing forth a genuine response."[4] These "contrivances" generally characterize poets whom Dickey finds false or less than complete. Yet his extensive comments about how writers fail also serve as his means for identifying the rare genuine poets.

Dickey deplores merely elegant language, or language that announces itself as "poetic"; he hates the dishonesty of false sufferers, and he abhors the condescension of intellectual elitism. These flaws, he asserts, prevent genuine connections among poet, poem, and reader: "If the reader does not, through the writing, gain a new, intimate, and vital perspective on his own life as a human being, there is no poem at all."[5]

The problem of false, "poetic" language abounds in contemporary verse, Dickey believes. He calls Robert Duncan, for example, "one of the most unpityingly pretentious poets I have ever come across. . . . As he keeps telling us, he is a mystic, which of course allows him to say anything in any order."[6] "Mark Strand's poetry strikes me as essentially silly, being a simple-minded kind of exercise in deliberate eccentricity."[7] Yet even when pretentiousness or eccentricity is replaced by real skill and ease in language, a danger exists:

James Merrill is the most graceful, attractive, and accomplished of the "elegants": the highly skilled, charming, agreeable craftsmen of the forties and fifties who promised most and delivered least. . . . One tires very quickly of the exquisite, nonvital kind of sensibility, and is inclined to yearn with increasing restiveness for precisely those qualities which Merrill, Anthony Hecht, and Richard Wilbur do not give.[8]

Dickey's objection to these obviously talented writers is that they appear to be more interested in smoothness of language, of tone, and of form than in depth of feeling. Consequently their skill becomes a limitation on their vision. Merrill, Hecht, and especially Wilbur produce the packaged poem that announces itself as poetry. But, Dickey states, "I do not wish to say anything in poetry *neatly*. That is the main trouble with Dick Wilbur's poetry: the sense of habitual dispatch. This is not only, in the end, tiresome, but even comes to seem a kind of poetical reflex. That is the wrong way to get a poem to behave."[9] If his craftsmanship, however admirable, becomes a reflex, then a poet's vision—his emotional and intellectual authenticity— may become unconvincing. The skill of the "elegant" poets, Dickey suggests, may serve as a barrier or mask separating writer from reader, and Dickey decries the gulf that consequently results.

When the mask is removed, as in the case of such "confessional" poets as Robert Lowell, W. D. Snodgrass, Anne Sexton, and Sylvia Plath, Dickey detects a different kind of dishonesty:

My complaint against the poets of personal complaint is not that they are confessional . . . but that they are not confessional enough. They are slickly confessional; they are glib. They do not really offer the "real life"—as opposed to the "literary life"—they purport to do; they are astonishingly literary—and here I mean literary in the bad sense—despite their insistence on "ordinary life."[10]

In Dickey's view these poets—particularly Plath and Sexton— illustrate perhaps the worst of all literary pretensions: a self-conscious pose of suffering. In "The Firebombing," Dickey writes that when some families are burned alive, "The others try to feel / For them. Some can, it is often said." His apparently calm statement is really an anguished comment about *wanting* to feel compassion, or guilt, but finally and honestly acknowledging that he is unable wholly to do so. Yet, as he notes,

It's fashionable to talk about guilt in poems, like Sylvia Plath feeling guilty over the slaughter of the Jews. She didn't have anything to do with it. She can be *sorry*, but guilt is more personal than that; it has to do with something you have *done*, or could have done and didn't. It's a literary convention for her. To have guilt, you've got to earn guilt, but sometimes when you earn it, you don't feel the guilt you ought to have. And that's what "The Firebombing" is about.[11]

Dickey loathes this easy assumption of guilt, for it both trivializes the horror of the Holocaust and discredits Plath's stance as a poet. Her painless, fashionable identification with the Jewish dead creates serious doubts about the emotional authenticity of her work.

The failures of language, of form, and of vision contribute to a poet's lack of success with an audience. Dickey feels the verse of I. A. Richards illustrates a specific kind of difficulty:

Its overingenuity seems to me just that, and this quality is, I strongly suspect, the main reason for the decline in audience that Richards deplores. . . . Too many potential readers think that it isn't worth all that trouble. . . . I can't shake off the conviction that verse so written—verse like Richards's and Empson's—has done much to drive the audience underground, into the beatnik coffeehouses, with its specialized references, its recondite images from physics and semantics . . .

all things that notes must be required to "fill the reader in" on and without which the meanings—even *one* of them—can't be grasped or even guessed at. . . . His poems *illustrate* as few others do why poetry is little read by others than poets, friends and relatives of poets, and captive audiences such as reviewers.[12]

Dickey holds that the genuine literary work and artist transcend the confines of the academy and are instead centered in experience; Richards, however, seems to regard literature as a kind of intellectual exercise, which perpetuates the notion that poetry can appeal only to the learned. He thus—like T. S. Eliot—limits the range of his vision and his audience. Dickey, on the other hand, includes his reader in his vision. The writer's purpose is to intensify experience:

The poet must evoke a world that is realer than real: his work must result in an intensification of qualities, you might say, that we have all observed and lived, but the poet has observed and lived most deeply of all. This world is so real that the experienced world is transfigured and intensified, through the poem, into *itself*, a deeper *itself*, a more characteristic *itself*. If a man can make words do this, he is a poet. Only men who do this *are* poets.[13]

The genuine poet moves his audience emotionally and intellectually.

In his excellent 1979 lecture, "The Water-Bug's Mittens: Ezra Pound: What We Can Use," Dickey notes that Pound is of great "practical" value to other poets, for his influence appears everywhere in American poetry: "Pound's presence is so pervasive that a contemporary poet cannot put down a single word, cannot hear, even far off or far back in his head, a cadence, a rhythm, without the suspicion that Pound has either suggested it or is in the process of causing him to accept it or reject it."[14] For these contributions Pound is to be valued, yet he also provides both "enormous, scattered, dismayingly wrong-headed and dazzlingly right-headed learning."[15] But finally Dickey believes Pound fails because he cannot bond with his audience.

One of the main troubles with it [*The Cantos*] is its lack of actual concern with people. Every person that Pound brings to our attention is an *example* of something: that is to say, a symbol, an effigy, a stand-in for an abstraction. . . . there is a distressing erector-set mechanicalness about *The Cantos*, a complex in-group snobbery, a very off-putting air of contemptuous intellectual superiority, and I'm afraid one part of me will never get over it.[16]

Robert Penn Warren and Theodore Roethke embody Dickey's concept of ideal poets. Warren, for example, is able to provide "the *formal* intensity of art, the sense of the thing done right."[17] At the same time, Dickey asserts that "one is concerned finally less with this than with the knowledge that these poems invest us with the greatest and most exacting of all human powers: that of discovering and defining what we must be, within the thing that we are."[18] Discussing Warren in his essay "The Weathered Hand and Silent Space," Dickey defines what he calls "pure" and "impure" poets:

If Wallace Stevens—to take Warren's most notable and obvious opposite—is "pure," Warren is impure; if Stevens changes reality by changing the angle of his eye, Warren fixes himself into it in wonder, horror, loathing, joy, but above all with unflinching involvement. . . . Warren encounters it nakedly, and without pretense, dallying, or skillful frivolity.[19]

Dickey's metaphor for Warren's poetic voice is his "farmer's hard, work-cramped hand."[20] His is a hand—and voice—that rejects the merely elegant, graceful phrase in favor of a rough-hewn power resulting from his *"angst,* a kind of radiant metaphysical terror, projected outward into the natural world. . . . He is direct, scathingly honest, and totally serious about what he feels. . . . [Yet] he is fully aware of the Longinian pit that yawns for those who strive for Sublimity and fail to attain it.[21] Warren's power forces readers' involvement with his poetry, for "he wounds deeply, and he connects deeply; he strikes in at blood-level and gut-level, with all the force and authority of time, darkness and distance themselves, and of the Nothingness beyond nothingness."[22]

It is this commitment to the Sublime—achieved not through refinement but through the raw, jagged power of language, form, and vision—that Dickey feels is the mark of the genuinely gifted poet. These same qualities occur in the work of Theodore Roethke, one of the "great Empathizers" whose forceful vision awakens a reader's inner life:

Roethke . . . can change your life not by telling but by showing, not from the outside but from within, by the lively and persistently mysterious means of inducing you to believe that you were *meant* to perceive and know things. . . . Roethke's marvelous sensuous apprehension of the natural world . . . and his total commitment to both his vision and to the backbreaking craft of verse [are compelling traits]. . . . I . . . was struck by the increasing mastery of form as well as by the reckless willingness to throw everything out the window and start over again, get back to first things, to primal sources, to risk sounding ridiculous and awkward in the quest of things that cannot be made to appear smooth and easy. I was moved also by the deepening of perception and the steady increase in joyousness as the man himself became older.[23]

This passage contains keys to Dickey's definition of what poets and poetry should be. Roethke's mastery of form, once accomplished, does not become an end in itself, as form seemingly does for Merrill, Hecht, and Wilbur. Rather, this writer is willing to risk further explorations in order to achieve an even more intense perception of his "primal sources." And his willingness to change, to grow, may cause him to "risk sounding ridiculous and awkward"—a risk the "elegant" craftsmen would presumably never take. Yet this daring allows the genuine poet to awaken readers into their own personal inner lives. Such writing is not "smooth and easy" but instead arduous, rough-hewn, reaching for the Sublime.

DICKEY AS CRITIC

It should be apparent that in defining what is suspect and what is genuine in poetry, Dickey's criticism outlines his own poetic theory. His honesty may cause him to be perceived by some as a "hatchet man," but in fact it suggests the seriousness with which he approaches his task. He is a poet who cares deeply about his art, who consequently insists on the highest possible standards. Richard Kostelanestz's 1965 statement calling Dickey America's finest critic of poetry may be even more accurate now than it was over twenty years ago.

Notes

1. Richard Kostelanetz, "Flyswatter and Gadfly," *Shenandoah* 16 (Spring 1965) 92–95.

2. Richard J. Calhoun, "Whatever Happened to the Poet-Critic?" *Southern Literary Journal* ns 1 (Autumn 1968) 75–88.

3. Calhoun 75.

4. *The Suspect in Poetry* (Madison, MN: Sixties Press, 1964) 9.

5. *The Suspect in Poetry* 9.

6. *Babel to Byzantium* 173.

7. *Sorties* 97.

8. *Babel to Byzantium* 97–98.

9. *Sorties* 45.

10. *Sorties* 190–91.

11. *Self-Interviews* 137.

12. *Babel to Byzantium* 180–81.

13. *Babel to Byzantium* 16–17.

14. *Night Hurdling* 30.

15. *Night Hurdling* 29.

16. *Night Hurdling* 43.

17. *Babel to Byzantium* 77.

UNDERSTANDING JAMES DICKEY

18. *Babel to Byzantium* 77.
19. *Night Hurdling* 54–55.
20. *Night Hurdling* 53.
21. *Night Hurdling* 52–53.
22. *Night Hurdling* 55.
23. *Babel to Byzantium* 149–50.

BIBLIOGRAPHY

This list of James Dickey's separate publications includes all books from trade publishers. Many limited editions, keepsakes, and similar collector's items of Dickey's works have been produced. Only the most important of these materials have been included in this list.

Books

Into the Stone and Other Poems, in *Poets of Today VII*, ed. John Hall Wheelock. New York: Scribner's, 1960. (Fifteen of the 24 poems are reprinted in *Poems 1957–1967*.) Poetry.

Drowning with Others. Middletown, CT: Wesleyan University Press, 1962. (Twenty-five of the 36 poems are reprinted in *Poems 1957–1967*.) Poetry.

Helmets. Middletown, CT: Wesleyan University Press, 1964. (Twenty-two of the 27 poems are reprinted in *Poems 1957–1967*.) Poetry.

The Suspect in Poetry. Madison, MN: Sixties Press, 1964. Reviews/Essays.

Buckdancer's Choice. Middletown, CT: Wesleyan University Press, 1965. (All 22 poems are reprinted in *Poems 1957–1967*.) Poetry.

BIBLIOGRAPHY

Poems 1957–1967. Middletown, CT: Wesleyan University Press, 1967. (*Falling*, which makes up the final section of *Poems 1957–1967*, had its first book appearance here.) Poetry.

Spinning the Crystal Ball. Washington, DC: Library of Congress, 1967. Essay.

Babel to Byzantium: Poets & Poetry Now. New York: Farrar, Straus, & Giroux, 1968. Reprinted with new Afterword, New York: Ecco Press, 1981. Reviews/Essays.

Metaphor as Pure Adventure. Washington, DC: Library of Congress, 1968. Essay.

Poems. Melbourne, Australia: Sun Books, 1968. Poetry.

Deliverance. Boston: Houghton Mifflin, 1970. Novel.

Self-Interviews, recorded and ed. Barbara and James Reiss. Garden City: Doubleday, 1970. Essays.

The Eye-Beaters, Blood, Victory, Madness, Buckhead and Mercy. Garden City: Doubleday, 1970. Poetry.

Stolen Apples, by Yevgeny Yevtushenko. Garden City: Doubleday, 1971. Includes 12 poems adapted by Dickey.

Sorties. Garden City: Doubleday, 1971. Journal/Essays.

Jericho: The South Beheld. Birmingham, AL: Oxmoor House, 1974.

The Zodiac. Garden City: Doubleday, 1976. Limited edition of 61 numbered and signed copies, each of which contains one page of the revised working draft of the poem, Bloomfield Hills, MI and Columbia, SC: Bruccoli Clark, 1976. Poem.

God's Images: The Bible, a New Vision. Birmingham, AL: Oxmoor House, 1977. Essays.

Tucky the Hunter. New York: Crown, 1978. Children's poem.

The Strength of Fields. Garden City: Doubleday, 1979. Poetry.

The Early Motion: Drowning with Others and Helmets. Middletown, CT: Wesleyan University Press, 1981. (Reprints the two volumes of poems with a new preface by Dickey.) Poetry.

BIBLIOGRAPHY

Falling, May Day Sermon, and Other Poems. Middletown, CT:
    Wesleyan University Press, 1981. (Reprints "May Day Sermon"
    and the poems of *Falling* with a new preface by Dickey.) Poetry.
Puella. Garden City: Doubleday, 1982. Poetry.
The Central Motion: Poems, 1968–1979. Middletown, CT:
    Wesleyan University Press, 1983. (Reprints *The Eye-Beaters,
    Blood, Victory, Madness, Buckhead and Mercy; The Zodiac;* and
    The Strength of Fields with a new preface by Dickey.) Poetry.
*Night Hurdling: Poems, Essays, Conversations, Commencements,
    and Afterwords.* Columbia, SC and Bloomfield Hills, MI:
    Bruccoli Clark, 1983.

Uncollected Introductions/Forewords—Selected

Foreword. *Of Poetry and Poets,* Richard Eberhart. Urbana:
    University of Illinois Press, 1979.
"Boys of the River-God." Introduction, *The Adventures of Tom
    Sawyer and Adventures of Huckleberry Finn,* Mark Twain. New
    York: New American Library, 1979.
Foreword. *Oystering: A Way of Life,* Charles L. Wyrick, Jr.
    Charleston, SC: Carolina Art Association, 1983.

Uncollected Periodical Appearances—Selected

"Cahill Is Blind," *Esquire* February 1976: 67–69, 139–144. Fiction.
"Frantic to Overtake Himself," review of *Jack: A Biography of Jack
    London* by Andrew Sinclair. *New York Times Book Review* 18
    September 1977: 7, 44.
"Compassionate Classicist," review of *This Blessed Earth* and
    Afternoon: Amaganset Beach by John Hall Wheelock. *New York
    Times Book Review* 10 December 1978: 14, 56–57.
"Selling His Soul to the Devil by Day . . . and Buying It Back by
    Night," *T.V. Guide,* 14 July 1979: 18–20. Essay.

BIBLIOGRAPHY

Films
A Poetry Experience on Film: Lord, Let Me Die but Not Die Out. Chicago: Encyclopaedia Britannica, 1970. About Dickey.

Screenplays
Deliverance. Warner Brothers, 1972. Carbondale and Edwardsville: Southern Illinois University Press, 1982.
Call of the Wild. Charles Fries, 1976.

Other
"Notes for Works in Progress," *Pages,* 1 (Detroit: Gale Research, 1976): 9–19. Fiction.

Selected Works about Dickey

Bibliographies/Checklists

Ashley, Franklin B. *James Dickey: A Checklist.* Columbia, SC and Detroit, MI: Bruccoli Clark/Gale Research, 1972. Primary.

Covel, Robert C. "Bibliography." *James Dickey Newsletter,* 1. 1 (Fall 1984): 15–27. Primary and secondary.

Elledge, Jim. *James Dickey: A Bibliography, 1947–1974.* Metuchen, NJ: Scarecrow Press, 1979. Primary and secondary.

_____. "James Dickey: A Supplementary Bibliography, 1975–1980: Part I." *Bulletin of Bibliography* 38 (April–June 1981): 92–100, 104. Primary and secondary.

_____. "James Dickey: A Supplementary Bibliography, 1975–1980: Part II." *Bulletin of Bibliography* 38 (July–September 1981): 150–55. Primary and secondary. Covering material from 1947–1980, Elledge's annotated bibliographies are the most thorough and reliable in print.

BIBLIOGRAPHY

Fritz, Donald E. and Patricia De La Fuente. "James Dickey: An Updated Checklist of Scholarship, 1975–1978." *James Dickey: Splintered Sunlight: Interview, Essays, and Bibliography.* Ed. Patricia De La Fuente. Edinburg, TX: Pan American University, 1979. Secondary.

Glancey, Eileen K. *James Dickey: The Critic as Poet: An Annotated Bibliography with an Introductory Essay.* Troy, NY: Whitson, 1971. Primary and secondary.

Hill, Robert W. "James Dickey: A Checklist." *James Dickey: The Expansive Imagination: A Collection of Essays,* ed. Richard J. Calhoun. Deland, FL: Everett/Edwards, 1973. Primary and Secondary.

Vannatta, Dennis. "A Checklist of Secondary Sources." *The Imagination as Glory: The Poetry of James Dickey.* Ed. Bruce Weigl and T. R. Hummer. Urbana and Chicago: University of Illinois Press, 1984.

Books

Calhoun, Richard J., ed. *James Dickey: The Expansive Imagination: A Collection of Critical Essays.* Deland, FL: Everett/Edwards, 1973. Fifteen essays, most of them previously published in journals, and a checklist of primary and secondary sources. Contributors include some of the most influential Dickey critics.

Calhoun, Richard J. and Robert W. Hill. *James Dickey.* Boston: Twayne, 1983. The first book-length study of Dickey's work through *Puella.* Calhoun and Hill provide an intelligent and thorough analysis of Dickey as a neo-romantic who "unabashedly uses himself as his own exemplar." They assert that his major

BIBLIOGRAPHY

source of "new power and insight" is an "imaginative interchange" between poet and nature. To gain a degree of glory, the writer must engage in the proper artistic, philosophical, and physical relationship with nature, a relationship which results from this interchange.

De La Fuente, Patricia, ed. *James Dickey: Splintered Sunlight: Interview, Essays, and Bibliography.* Edinburgh, TX: Pan American University, 1979. Includes an interview with Dickey, five new essays, a checklist to scholarship 1975–1978, and a sampling of student responses to the poet's visit to Pan American University.

Lieberman, Laurence. *The Achievement of James Dickey: A Comprehensive Selection of His Poems with a Critical Introduction.* Glenview, IL: Scott, Foresman, 1968. The first extended discussion of Dickey's poetry, focusing particularly on the fusion of celebration and terror in his work.

Weigl, Bruce and T. R. Hummer, eds. *The Imagination as Glory: The Poetry of James Dickey.* Urbana and Chicago: University of Illinois Press, 1984. A well-balanced collection of previously published essays, providing the "most characteristic statements within the body of Dickey's criticism." Included are a checklist of secondary sources and two essays by Dickey—"The Energized Man" and "The Imagination as Glory."

Selected Articles, Interviews, Parts of Books

Arnett, David L. "An Interview with James Dickey." *Contemporary Literature* 16 (Summer 1975): 286–300. Dickey discusses the rite of passage motif in *Deliverance* and offers information about the novel's origin. He also comments on some of his poems, particularly those in *The Eye-Beaters.*

BIBLIOGRAPHY

Bartlett, Lee and Hugh Witemeyer. "Ezra Pound and James Dickey: A Correspondence and a Kinship." *Paideuma*, 2 (Fall 1982): 290–312. Reprints and discusses letters between the two poets from 1955 to 1958. The correspondence confirms Dickey's later statement in "The Water-Bug's Mittens" that communicating with Pound was like talking to "your own crazy, intelligent father."

Bennett, Ross. " 'The Firebombing': A Reappraisal." *American Literature* 52 (November 1980): 430–48. Identifying the quest for self-discovery at the heart of the poem, Bennett calls "The Firebombing" Dickey's most important work and perhaps the best American poem since 1945.

Berry, David C., Jr. "Harmony with the Dead: James Dickey's Descent into the Underworld." *Southern Quarterly* 12 (April 1974): 233–44. Shows how the poet functions as an Orpheus-like figure moving between the worlds of the living and the dead. Reprinted in *The Imagination as Glory*.

Bloom, Harold. "James Dickey: From 'The Other' through *The Early Motion*." *The Southern Review*, 21 (Winter 1985), 63–78. Identifies mythological and other literary influences in "The Other" and in Dickey's first three collections as a whole.

Bly, Robert ("Crunk"). "The Collapse of James Dickey." *Sixties*, 9 (Spring 1967), 70–79. Bly's comments about Dickey's apparent enthusiasm for war sparked a literary feud that helped define both writiers' philosophical/aesthetic stances. See *Self-Interviews* 72; *Sorties* 196–98.

Calhoun, Richard J. "Whatever Happened to the Poet-Critic?" *Southern Literary Journal*, 1 (Autumn 1968): 75–88. In one of the best essays on Dickey as critic Calhoun focuses on the central theme of *Babel to Byzantium*—that each poet has his own vision, his Byzantium, to fulfill. Reprinted in *The Expansive Imagination*.

BIBLIOGRAPHY

Davison, Peter. "The Difficulties of Being Major: The Poetry of Robert Lowell and James Dickey." *Atlantic Monthly,* October 1967: 116–21. Calling Dickey and Lowell the most important poets of their time, Davison contrasts Lowell's movement toward the city—toward civilization and its structured institutions—with Dickey's movement into the wilderness and its instructions for man. Reprinted in *The Expansive Imagination.*

DeMott, Benjamin. "The 'More Life' School and James Dickey." *The Saturday Review,* (28 March 1970): 25–26, 38. Slightly acerbic in tone, DeMott views Dickey as a larger-than-life figure who aims for expansive rather than limiting subjects and themes.

Friedman, Norman. "The Wesleyan Poets, II: The Formal Poets, 2." *Chicago Review* 19 (January 1966): 55–67, 72. Analyzes key images and themes—the "wound motif," for example—in Dickey's work.

Greiner, Donald J. "The Harmony of Bestiality in James Dickey's *Deliverance.*" *South Carolina Review* 5 (December 1972): 43–49. While focusing on the novel's revelation of savagery behind man's civilized mask, Greiner provides an excellent discussion of critical responses to *Deliverance.*

Guillory, Daniel L. "Water Magic in the Poetry of James Dickey." *English Language Notes* 8 (December 1970): 131–37. Shows how Dickey's water symbols embody both life and death.

Heyen, William. "A Conversation with James Dickey." *Southern Review* 9 (January 1973): 135–56. This interview probes Dickey's views of death and the Other and elicits background comments on "The Performance," "The Heaven of Animals," "The Bee," and "Sled Burial, Dream Ceremony." Reprinted as "In Louisiana" in *Night Hurdling.*

BIBLIOGRAPHY

Hill, Robert W. "James Dickey, Comic Poet." *The Expansive Imagination* 143–55. Hill defines Dickey's comic vision as a means of gaining a balance between "terror and exaltation" in his assessment of life.

Howard, Richard. "On James Dickey." *Partisan Review* 33 (Summer 1966): 414–28, 479–86. This early essay provides a remarkably thorough analysis of subjects, themes, and symbols in Dickey's poetry through *Buckdancer's Choice*.

Italia, Paul G. "Love and Lust in James Dickey's *Deliverance*." *Modern Fiction Studies* 21 (Summer 1975): 203–13. Finding a pattern in the novel of "struggle, copulation, and death," this essay plots the balancing of sexual act and retribution, of crime and countercrime.

Kostelanetz, Richard. "Flyswatter and Gadfly." *Shenadoah* 16 (Spring 1965): 92–95. This review of *The Suspect in Poetry* is one of the earliest tributes to Dickey as critic. Reprinted in *The Expansive Imagination*.

Lieberman, Laurence. "The Worldly Mystic." *Hudson Review* 20 (Autumn 1967): 513–20. An important essay discussing the dual impulses in Dickey's poetry toward the real and the mystical, the outer and the inner worlds. Reprinted in *The Expansive Imagination*.

———. "Notes on James Dickey's Style." *Far Point* 2 (Spring-Summer 1969): 57–63. Lieberman shows how Dickey's style assists his "heightened reportage" of experience.

Mills, Ralph J. *Creation's Very Self: On the Personal Element in Recent American Poetry* (Fort Worth: Texas Christian University, 1969), pp. 3–5, 18. Mills provides an excellent discussion of how contemporary American poets, including Dickey, have rejected

BIBLIOGRAPHY

T. S. Eliot's notion that poetry should be an escape from the writer's personality and emotion. Instead, they have placed the Self at the center of their work.

————. "The Poetry of James Dickey." *Triquarterly* 11 (Winter 1968): 231–42. Mills's essay is among the most important in defining Dickey's themes and techniques, particularly his use of dream, sleep, and illusion imagery to achieve transformation. Reprinted in *The Imagination as Glory*.

Mizejewski, Linda. " Shamanism toward Confessionalism: James Dickey, Poet." *Georgia Review* 32 (Summer 1978): 409–19. Attributing the failure of *The Zodiac* to Dickey's overreaching his vision, Mizejewski ends with a call for the poet to return to the subject matter and techniques of his earlier volumes. Reprinted in *The Imagination as Glory*.

Nemerov, Howard. "Poems of Darkness and a Specialized Light." *Sewanee Review* 71 (January-March 1963): 99–104. This early essay was the first to identify the relationship between darkness/moonlight and visionary powers in Dickey's poetry. Reprinted in *The Imagination as Glory*.

Norman, Geoffrey. "*Playboy* Interview: James Dickey." *Playboy* November 1973: 81–82, 86, 89, 92, 94, 212–216. Dickey comments on his war experience and discusses his views of nature and the poet's role in society.

Oates, Joyce Carol. "Out of Stone, Into Flesh: The Imagination of James Dickey." *Modern Poetry Studies* 5 (Autumn 1974): 97–144. Seeing Dickey's Self as an embodiment of modern man's frustration and rage, Oates regards the poet as relentlessly honest in exploring the Self and as obsessed with a "need to seek and to define." Reprinted in *The Imagination as Glory*.

BIBLIOGRAPHY

O'Neil, Paul, "The Unlikeliest Poet." *Life* 22 July 1966: 68–70, 72–74, 77–79. This essay for a general audience discusses Dickey's background and nonliterary interests as well as his writing and teaching activities.

Sloan, Thomas O. "The Open Poem Is a Now Poem: Dickey's May Day Sermon." *Literature as Revolt and Revolt as Literature.* Minneapolis: University of Minnesota Press, 1969. An analysis of "May Day Sermon" pointing out the poem's association of females with natural, unrestrained impulses and of males with artificial, repressive systems. Sloan shows that in this work passion triumphs over restraint. Reprinted in *The Expansive Imagination.*

Smith, Dave. "The Strength of James Dickey." *Poetry* 137 (March 1981): 349–58. This review labels *The Zodiac* an impressive failure; it finds in *The Strength of Fields* Dickey's increased awareness of his own mortality accompanied by a sheer sense of joy at his larger world and his diminishing impatience with the constraints of form. Reprinted in *The Imagination as Glory.*

Strange, William C. "To Dream, To Remember: James Dickey's *Buckdancer's Choice.*" *Northwest Review* 7 (Fall-Winter 1965–66): 33–42. A good discussion of Dickey's use of dreams to perceive his world.

Weatherby, H. L. "The Way of Exchange in James Dickey's Poetry." *Sewanee Review* 74 (July-September 1966): 669–80. Perhaps the most influential treatment of Dickey's poetry, Weatherby's essay defines the method by which Dickey exchanges identity with the Other—inanimate objects, animals, and human beings—to achieve a new perspective on his world. Reprinted in *The Expansive Imagination* and *The Imagination as Glory.*

BIBLIOGRAPHY

Newsletter

James Dickey Newsletter, ed. Joyce Pair. Dunwoody, GA: Dekalb
  Community College, Fall 1984–.

Journal

South Carolina Review 10 (April 1978). Special issue devoted to
  Dickey.

INDEX

INDEX

INDEX

INDEX

INDEX

INDEX

INDEX

INDEX

2   2/69

2 11/91